P9-DDO-942

CRAPS

HOW TO PLAY TO WIN

by

EFFEMAR

A Scientific Study Based on One Million Rolls of the Dice

VANTAGE PRESS • NEW YORK

WASHINGTON • HOLLYWOOD • TORONTO

FIRST EDITION

Published by Vantage Press, Inc.
120 West 31st Street, New York 1, N. Y.
Manufactured in the United States of America
Library of Congress Catalog Card Number: 56-11196

Foreword

Over a million rolls of the dice were made in this study of the LAW OF AVERAGES, or of the LAW OF PROBABILITIES as applied to Games of Chance—in particular, to Craps. Many tens of thousands of these figures were tabulated and scientifically grouped according to their relations to other figures.

A careful analysis of these figures reveals how "chance" can largely be removed from a Game of Chance, be it Cards, Craps, or any game where two dice are used in the play.

In 1949, the Court of Common Pleas, Merced County, Ohio, ruled: "Bridge is a game of skill, not chance." This Court quoted an old North Carolina court decision to the effect that "games of skill are distinguished from games of chance in that the latter depend upon luck or chance, in which adroitness has no office at all." So "Chess, Checkers, and Bowling," it adds, "are games of skill." Many might disagree with this conclusion. One might impiously ask, "How about Poker?" for gamblers do not gamble.

However, in the light of this interpretation, the author fully believes he has reduced the Game of Craps to a Game of Skill, in which one can consistently win, whether he plays ten minutes or ten hours. Adroitness can figure beautifully in the Game of Craps.

When the ignorant and the uninformed engage in Games of Chance—which include Horse Racing—they are gambling. Even though informed with "scientific" records as in the latter "Sport," the bettor is still gambling. Horse Racing, legalized in a dozen states, and regarded as a legitimate business, is the greatest swindling racket permitted in the United States. Though masquerading under the euphonious title "Sport of Kings"—and of millionaires—nevertheless, from the standpoint of the public, it is a gigantic gambling game, in which those who bet stand less chance of winning then those who stand at a "Crap Table."

The author has handicapped over 350,000 horses and has recorded 1,000,000 rolls of the dice, so he can state positively—"*Playing Craps is less a gambling venture than is betting the races.*"

Thousands of Systems have been built upon the figures of Horse Racing, not one of which can guarantee a winner. Any System will pick some winners, but the very best can offer no sure thing. There is no more certainty in picking the winner in a race than there is in winning in one throw of the dice. In fact, the latter offers by far the better chance—to one who *knows*.

But in any event, over ninety percent of those who engage in these Games of Chance are losers. In Horse Racing, in most cases, only those who have something to sell—touts of every conceivable description—make money.

In a dozen or more of our states, Horse Racing is legalized. Craps is legalized in one state. Yet Craps is a game played *sub rosa* all over the United States, and in many instances it is protected by those in authority. It is the belief of the author that in Nevada, where Craps is legal gambling, the player is far better protected against dishonesty than are those who bet the Horse Races, with tracks close to all our great cities. It is astonishing to what length unscrupulous touts are able to go in deceiving a gullible public.

All gambling is unmoral. Why should one form be glorified, and another, less obnoxious, be prohibited?

This book is a scientific experimental study of the trends of given numbers as the dice are rolled. This book is without parallel in its analysis of the combinations of figures revealed by the rolling dice. It is not offered to the public with any intent to encourage gambling. On the contrary, it offers protection to those who, because of lack of knowledge, will gamble. As the Crap Game is legal in Nevada, this book is especially for those who play there.

It offers intellectual, educational entertainment to those who will demonstrate to themselves, with a pair of perfect dice, the conclusions arrived at.

The author makes no pretense of knowing all that is to be known about the roll of the dice, or the Game of Craps. The facts presented in this book must speak for themselves.

EFFEMAR

CONTENTS

PART THREE

LIST OF TABLES

The more a man knows

the better luck he has.

—Confucius

PART ONE

1—Chance or Luck

A prudent man foreseeth the evil, and hideth himself; but the simple pass on, and are punished.
PROVERB OF SOLOMON

Many pearls of wisdom dropped from the tongue of this Wise Man. Speaking of the vicissitudes of the sons of men, he said, "Time and chance happeneth to them all."

It is quite obvious that humans come into this world by chance, and considering the mortality on the highways and the multitude of lethal mechanisms about us, a goodly number make their exit in the same manner.

"This happened," "that happened," or "by chance" are common everyday expressions. Perhaps if we possessed the vision to see the invisible, these "happenings" might not prove to be chance. Inasmuch as we are not so equipped, chance figures very largely in human affairs.

There are very few certainties in this world other than death and taxes. In spite of any local famine, there always will be enough food, if properly distributed, to supply the entire world population. That the sun will rise and set, that the moon and stars will pursue their courses and always shine, are absolute certainties. But the rains, the winds, the sunshine and the temperature, all affecting human life, can be forecast only a few days in advance.

Before the growing season begins, the wisest of scientists cannot forecast whether the crops will be plentiful or scant; whether it will be a cold or wet season or not. So the farmer and the gardener "take a chance" as Solomon had observed in his experience, for he said, "In the morning sow thy seed, and in the evening withhold not thine hand; for thou knowest not whether shall prosper this or that, or whether they both shall be alike good,"—or bad, he might have added.

Beginning with seedtime, the farmer is ever gambling with the weather and pests, whether he will have a good crop or little, whether he will have good prices or suffer a loss. This same element, chance, enters into most of the activities of people. Hence the often-heard expression, "Life is just a gamble."

Inasmuch as "time and chance happeneth" to all mankind, the history of the race in all ages among all peoples reveals that the gambling spirit has played an important role in human affairs.

It is interesting to note the origin of the word "chance." It comes from the Latin, and literally means something falling—like dice. In the golden days of the Empire, the Romans were great gamblers, and they used dice. So chance and dice have a very close relationship.

There are over one hundred words in our language, more or less synonymous with chance, and they are so used in daily conversation to give expression to experiences and happenings. To one, chance may be fortuitous—to another, disastrous. Happen and happily both come from the noun "hap," which means chance.

In the beautiful romantic story of Ruth in the Bible (Ruth 2:3) the word "hap" is used, the only instance in the Scriptures. In Hebrew it meant "happened." As by chance Ruth gleaned in the fields of Boaz—and what a happy outcome!

Considering it more as a figure of speech than a reality, to many there appears to be a "Wheel of Fortune" shaping our destiny. Be this as it may, to the vast majority of mankind this wheel has never made a revolution.

The Chinese have a saying: "When fortune smiles, who doesn't? When fortune doesn't, who does?"

In every walk of life, be it business, professional, political, or actual gambling, the "prudent man" stands at the top. He studies, works hard, analyzes, plans carefully, and hence is able to "foresee" and "hide himself" at the right time. "The simple pass on," oblivious of any danger, "and are punished,"—and how!

An unlearned man may be very prudent. There are many such in all walks of life. A simple man may be a university graduate. In the above quotation, the "simple man" is one of gullibility and inexperience, though perhaps a very good man. His type figures largely among those who are given a "shakedown," or taken for a "sucker." They are the prey of touts, "gold brick" salesmen, and the confidence man. It is quite evident that Solomon had these classes in mind when he wrote another good proverb:

> *The simple believe every word; but the*
> *prudent man looketh well to his going.*

What is usually termed "just plain luck" or "chance," is ninety-five percent hard work and right thinking. Poor luck and failure are ninety-five percent ignorance and wrong thinking. Apropos of this is another proverb by the same Wise Man: "As he thinketh in his heart, so is he." (Prov. 23:7)

However, the prudent man can make mistakes in his judgment, as for instance the merchant when he overstocks and "is punished" by losses.

Action in real estate, and trading in stocks is speculation at any time, but particularly so at the peak of a boom, or in a depression. When the turnover is great, one so engaged is regarded as gambling, and particularly so is the one who trades "over the counter." He is the prey of the "Commission Man."

The prudent man can usually come out with a profit, the novice loses his shirt.

The brokerage house deals in percentages, buys or sells, and seldom is the loser. Likewise the banks. Also the legalized Gambling Banks, or Houses, or Clubs. The percentage is in their favor. They are said not to gamble. They seem to win most of the money that comes into their establishments.

2—"The Gambler Does Not Gamble"

An article in the *Reader's Digest* with this title arrested my attention some years ago. Never having given the subject any attention or consideration, this caption struck me as strange. After reading the article, I understood the writer's viewpoint.

While this statement can be taken with a little salt, it does represent a relative degree of accuracy. What it means is this: an expert at Cards, Roulette, Horse Racing, or dealing in the stock market is pretty sure of what he is doing, and invests his money accordingly. He does not expect to carry away a profit every day. The most expert is hardly foolish enough to take that position. But he knows that in the end he will be ahead. The merchant may lose heavily during the summer and fall, but the Christmas trade will pull him out of the red.

The majority of the great crowds that attend a Race Track on a given day are losers. And ninety-five percent of those who bet almost daily are losers at the end of the season.

Probably a larger percentage of those who play Craps day after day, are losers in the end. Only a few are prudent enough to stop with a good winning, and call it a day. Few have the self-control to do this. Greed and covetousness get the better of most people.

Over and over, I have seen men win two or three hundred dollars, sometimes in a few minutes, and collect it at the cashier's window. Perhaps in an hour or so they are back at the same table or at another. They start losing almost from the beginning. They make larger bets than at first. They increase their bets to make up for the loss of a losing streak. It isn't long before all the winnings have vanished—and more capital.

A hundred dollars, or two or three, in an hour, or even in fifteen minutes, is pretty easy money. However, very few are satisfied. They think perhaps they can make it a thousand.

There are times when "beginner's luck" may be the experience of one who for the first time visits the Race Track or plays at the Crap Table.

Two women went to the Santa Anita race track one afternoon "just for a lark." Each had a drink. They knew nothing at all about how to pick a winner. They decided they would put two dollars on the horse that had the strangest name of any on the card. The horse won and paid $160.

A man who did not know a Crap Table from a lunch counter, had the dice pushed to him for the first time. He made 27 passes and won $26. A "gambler" would have made a small fortune with such a chance. No one at a Crap Table can forecast whether a shooter will roll the dice 3 times or 40 times before he shoots out.

Here are two or three experiences that happened within an hour. I was using ten-cent chips in an experiment I was working out. A large woman, wearing a fine fur coat, stopped at my side and bought five dollars' worth of chips. They gave her 50. She was very voluble. Apparently she was enjoying the effect of a drink or two. As she put down 5 chips on "any Crap," she said, "My, I feel wonderful." She lost the first bet. She put down five more and won 35, and everyone at the table knew she had won.

In a few minutes it was her turn to shoot. I believe she must have made 40 rolls of the dice. She had an unusual number of Craps showing. In twenty minutes that woman walked away from the table with twenty-three silver dollars. She was not conscious of the fact that from 50 to more than 100 rolls of the dice may intervene between any two Craps. She played during a favorable streak—when the rhythm of the dice included Two, Three, and Twelve—but the dice were not following the LAW OF AVERAGES.

Very shortly after, a young woman stood in the same place. She bought five dollars' worth of ten-cent chips. As she tried to put the chips on the rail, she said, "I don't know a thing about this game. What shall I do?"

A Stickman said, "Here, lady, put some chips on the Hardways."

"What's that?" she asked.

He indicated it with his stick. She put chips there and on all the Craps and on Seven. Two won and she was given 60 chips. That put her far ahead. She repeated this wild placing of chips. In a few minutes she was over 100 chips ahead. She put three silver dollars in her bag. In ten minutes more all her chips were gone. She walked away, loser by two dollars.

Profits at a Crap Table are very elusive. One should quit when the quitting is good.

3—What About Luck and Chance?

In the dictionary these two words are synonymous and may be used interchangeably. However, long dissertations have been written on the part that luck plays in human life. It does seem to have a slight edge over "chance." At least, it sounds better.

In the matter of its application to material gain and profit, there is no difference in meaning. It is wistful wishing for material gain or riches that urges the multitude to "take a chance," or "try my luck" "for once." Solomon said, "Money answereth all things." Most people agree with this.

For these reasons, gambling is rampant all over these United States and most of the world in one form or another. Horse Racing, the greatest swindling racket in this country, probably exceeds all other forms of gambling in popularity.

In golf, playing for money at so much per hole, is a common practice all over the land. Some young men who are quite expert make a good living at this form of gambling.

A Gallup poll taken a few years ago revealed that forty-three million people gamble in some form. Naturally this poll was limited to adults, representing over half of those queried. Fifty-four percent were in favor of a national lottery. A lottery is unadulterated gambling.

Playing for money in Card Games is a common pastime with women who have little to occupy their afternoon hours. Many make all their pin money this way—others lose it all. Many women will not engage in a Card Game unless there are small stakes per point.

There is more real gambling among the laboring classes than among any other, both small and large wage earners. They want more money than they earn, so they risk what they have in ventures of which they are largely ignorant. They fondly believe that if they persist at it they will have a "streak of luck."

The prudent man does not trust to luck or chance. He works hard. He studies extensively. He experiments thoroughly, until he has perfected himself to achieve his objective.

Just recently a man who had spent thirty to forty years in poverty and hardships, searching the hills, and mountains, and valleys of California for mineral wealth, as a last effort came back to a desert valley he had scouted a score of years before. He made one more try at it, this time for oil. He found it. Now he is a millionaire. That was not luck, but the result of persistent hard work through years of fruitless toil and privation. Long experience had sharpened his powers of observation. Confucius was indeed wise when he said: "The more a man knows, the better luck he has."

Luck is just another term, in the vast majority of cases, for hard work. Through this comes knowledge. Knowledge is far more reliable than luck.

4—Origin of the Game of Craps

The origin of this popular game is shrouded in the mist of antiquity and uncertainty. From what information we have to go on, it dates back to the period of the Crusades, or the eleventh and twelfth centuries. From the facts at hand, it is an evolution from a gambling game called Hazards, according to the Oxford English Dictionary.

The word "dice" is Arabic in origin, as is also "hazards," though the latter is French, coming from the word "Hazart," or "Azarte," the name of a castle in Palestine, held by the Arabs and besieged by the Crusaders, most of whom were Britons. The soldiers played a game with dice through weeks and months while waiting for the starving Arabs to surrender.

It was a game of two dice in which the chances were complicated by a number of arbitrary rules. Any number could play the game. The soldiers carried the game back to England where it became very popular and for centuries it was called Hazards. In those days it was a more hazardous game than now. The term figures very extensively in the literature of that period. To take a hazard was to take a very great risk—and today we say "at all hazards."

So the word came to be used in many games in which there was the element of chance, or a hazard.

To make the pocket in billiards was a hazard. In this game there was a winning hazard and a losing hazard.

Tennis is by no means a modern game. In this game in those early days, the court into which the ball was served was a hazard, or on the hazard side.

In golf a bunker is a hazard, also, a ditch, water, sand, or a piece of bad ground, hence making it a game of chance.

In England when a patient got rid of his physician, "he hazarded much."

5—Dealing Scientifically with Games of Chance

Nearly every Game of Chance deals with figures, be it stocks, Horse Racing, Cards, Roulette, Dice or Craps. Figures do not lie. Figures give facts, and facts are the "brute beasts of the intellectual domain."

Mathematics is an exact science. Groups of figures can be reduced to rules for interpretation.

When certain groups of figures are used over and over, it necessarily follows that a given figure will continue to repeat itself with systematic regularity. Because of this, man has formulated a mathematical rule called the LAW OF AVERAGES, or the LAW OF PROBABILITIES. This so-called law is more clearly revealed if 12 figures are used a certain number of times, than if 36 or 100 figures are used the same number of times.

In games using 2 dice, such as Craps, 12 figures appear in the roll of the dice. These 12 figures constitute all the plays. In Roulette 36 figures are used, with 0 and 00 added.

While the LAW OF AVERAGES is revealed as clearly with 36 numbers, as with 12, the latter takes much less time for its expression. It is astonishing to note how the average of certain figures will assert itself. In Craps, the Numbers Three and Eleven are each made in 2 ways, or in 2 combinations. According to the LAW OF AVERAGES, both should appear about the same number of times, let us say, in 1,000 rolls. In one of my series of 6,000 rolls of the dice, both came exactly 329 times!

In this study of facts about numbers, and knowing that the LAW OF AVERAGES definitely will assert itself over and over again with various numbers of different combinations, men have formulated rules of procedure for themselves, to enable them to win in the Games of Chance. They learn how to make the LAW OF AVERAGES act as handmaiden to success, and they also learn how to defeat Mr. Percentage, who is always against the player in any commercial Game of Chance.

6—Can the Game of Craps Be Made Scientific?

The word "science" means "knowledge." Science also suggests truth. True knowledge of facts and figures enables one to formulate rules and principles. To this we apply the term "scientific."

There are experts with Cards who claim they play the game scientifically. They know they will win—in time. There are experts in Roulette who claim they play scientifically. They know they will win—if they adhere to their method. There are racing fans who will make a bet only after "scientifically" handicapping a race. All such players are patient, can wait, and are not worried.

In each of these cases, as to its being scientific, it is only relatively so. The race handicapper has more facts and figures to work on than the player in any other Game of Chance. Consequently, the matter of selecting a horse might seem to be more scientific than the Game of Craps or Roulette.

The facts will show that betting the races is a more hazardous Game of Chance than is Craps. An expert in Craps can make much more money in less time than the expert handicapper. In Horse Racing it is the touts, or those who have something to sell, who make the most money, not the ones who buy the touts' selections, and put their money on them.

Science means "knowledge." There is *one unknown central fact* in Craps, in Roulette, and in selecting a horse, which can positively not be determined. If it could be, then the element of chance would not exist. In this unknown lies the chance, the uncertainty of these plays, even to the expert. Hence, the great multitude of the uninformed, having anything to do with these alluring games, are engaged in unadulterated gambling.

Put it down in your mind, once and for all, that there is no one so expert in rolling the dice that he can tell before the dice leave his fingers what number will show up at the end of the roll. No one can throw Sevens or Craps or Hardways at will. This challenging statement is predicated upon honesty in a legalized game, using perfectly machined dice. The Crap Tables have a perfect protection against any tricks in shooting the cubes.

Likewise, in Roulette no one can predict what number will receive the rolling ball.

Hence the expert does not count to any extent on luck or chance to win any game. He proceeds as scientifically as possible and follows his own rules. Therefore, to achieve a good profit in a Game of Chance, he has to put in long hours of preparation, give attention to detail, and make countless experiments, record his findings, then formulate rules of procedure, and finally finish up by long, possibly expensive, practice. Here, as elsewhere, experience is the best teacher. All this preparation takes considerable time. In this way Craps becomes a Game of Skill.

7—Rhythm and Cycles

Before finishing 100,000 rolls of the dice and recording the figures in books, I had come to the conclusion that there is a certain rhythm in the movement of the figures the dice roll up. I have also come to the conclusion that the volume of figures in the roll of the dice moves in cycles. The former may change in a few minutes. The latter involves thousands of rolls. Suffice it to say here, I believe the *rhythm in the roll of the dice may be broken,* and is frequently broken, but the *cycles* move slowly.

In both of these changes, there is a change in regularity so that certain numbers do not come at a time when they should by the LAW OF AVERAGES.

Hence it follows in any given 100 rolls of the dice, more or less (say at the time you begin to play), the LAW OF AVERAGES may not be followed at all. This is a feature in the game that no one can predict or alter. This may have an important bearing on your success or failure.

For instance, 70 rolls may intervene between 2 Sevens, when 6 to 7 is the average. On the other hand I have had 10 Sevens turning up in 23 rolls. Eleven has an average of 1 in 17 rolls. I have made 183 rolls between Elevens. Twelve appears once in 35 rolls. I have had over 600 rolls between appearances of the Number Twelve.

The expert becomes aware of this change and shapes his play accordingly. A novice cannot do this. The expert will follow the trend of the dice and not go against it. Or he will lay off or go to another table.

When dice roll in rhythm, the different numbers turning up on the Layout in a gambling House must appear more or less with certain regularity in order to establish the LAW OF AVERAGES.

The combinations that can be formed in the most ways naturally must come more often.

In 500 rolls, or 1,000, or 10,000, Number Seven will show up approximately once in every 6½ rolls, varying 1 roll more or less in these cycles.

Moreover, I have proved to my own satisfaction in the tabulation of thousands of rolls that a Seven should appear after *certain numbers* in quite regular fashion. When a Six or Eight, or some other number appears, when a Seven should normally be expected, the rhythm may be broken, and the shooter may roll 15, 20, 30, or even 50 rolls before a Seven wins or loses for the entire crowd at the table.

It is my conviction that the rhythm is more likely to be changed when a shooter is ruled by the superstition that he is more likely to "make the Point" or throw a Hardway, or a Seven, if he throws the dice with the violence of pitching a baseball. Also, if the energy of his throw causes one of the dice to leave the table or land "in the wood," with change of dice, the rhythm of that certain succession of numbers is broken.

To many this may sound like sheer nonsense. However, it is not. If you watch the roll of the numbers, you will grasp this point in time.

A player who is betting "big money" should have an understanding with the House that if a die leaves the table he has the right to remove all his chips until the rhythm is again established. At the very least, he should see that the dice are not changed.

If one has a certain plan of play based upon definite numbers and the rhythm is going against his play, as it easily can in Craps, a change of dice or moving to another table may correct this. There a different cycle is moving with the dice.

If the rhythm is favorable to your method, you win. If it changes, you doubtless will have to go into a mild progression to win, and then you must watch your step.

A Crap Table may be crowded for an hour or more because the players are winning, or seesawing back and forth, hoping they will win. In a few minutes, the table may be almost vacant, except for added shills. The crowd has gone to another table that promises better returns.

I stood at a table when a "Hot Wind" was blowing (meaning a shooter who throws 30 to 50 rolls before a Seven brings a decision). A young man stood at my side with two dollars in his hand, just as this shooter began. He placed his money on the Front Line (also deceptively marked the "Win Line"). A Natural came. He won. He left the money on and won again. He placed a "Come" bet and won. Then he began placing five-dollar bets. The shooter made a number of Passes and "Points." When he finally rolled a Seven, the young man was ahead $75. He said to me, "I guess I better quit." He was the exception to the usual player and winner.

Following this shooter, several Sevens came in quick succession after 2 to 4 rolls and no Points being made. The table was deserted in ten minutes. Many had lost all their winnings. This statement proves the point, which will be repeated over and over in these pages, viz: a long series of rolls between Sevens is usually followed by 2, 3, or up to 10 short plays of 2 to 5 or 6 rolls with no Point being made. The same fact holds true with Elevens or Craps. One hundred rolls may intervene between 2 Elevens, and then 5 or 6 may appear in 50 rolls.

In Craps, a winning streak is sure to be followed by a reverse. There is a change in the rhythm. Numbers out of the usual order are appearing, perhaps Five, Six, Eight are repeating over and over to the disgust of the one playing the Field. Or another group of numbers, as Four, Nine, Ten, are coming up persistently. This change of rhythm may come in ten minutes, in half an hour, or longer. It is inevitable. This may be the time for you to make a change, take a rest, or go to another Club.

8—The Dice

Dice are used in many Games of Chance. In this book only Craps will be considered. Also, only the points essential to winning will be considered.

To play for profit it is not essential to memorize all the percentages of the different combinations the two dice will make. Regardless of what feature one plays, the odds and percentages are against the player and in favor of the House.

To remember the odds is important. The odds are all figured according to the relative frequency with which a given combination will appear according to the number of ways that combination is made.

It is easy to understand that a combination that can be made in only 1 way, is not going to appear nearly as frequently as one that can be made in 6 ways, or 5 ways, or 4 ways. Good sense would naturally steer one away from risking money on a 35 to 1 play.

In the Game of Craps 2 dice are used. In states where the game is legalized, each cube used is claimed to be geometrically perfect or machined so perfectly that there is not supposed to be more than one ten-thousandth of an inch variation in the 6 sides.

The 6 sides are numbered One, Two, Three, Four, Five, Six. These numbers are flush with the surface, and not sunken, as nonprofessional dice are. This manner of placing the numbers contributes to a perfectly balanced die (which, incidentally, is the correct word for one of a pair of dice).

The edges are sharp and make perfect angles on all sides. The Gaming Houses seem to be very particular in removing dice from use that have the slightest roughening of the edge or corners. To examine the dice seems to be one of the chief functions of the ever-present Pit-Boss or the Box-Boss. This scrutiny contributes to an honest roll of the dice over the smooth table layout. With the average of small bettors at these tables, there is no doubt that the dice used are as described.

Each die has 6 sides and 6 numbers. These 12 numbers on a pair can make *11 different combinations,* and the dice combine in *36 ways.*

Note the following table. To be successful, a Crap player should know these *36 ways, forwards and backwards.*

COMBINATIONS AND NUMBER OF WAYS TO MAKE EACH

Number		*Ways*	*Manner*
2	made in	1	1-1
3	" "	2	2-1, 1-2
4	" "	3	3-1, 2-2, 1-3
5	" "	4	4-1, 1-4, 3-2, 2-3
6	" "	5	5-1, 1-5, 3-3, 4-2, 2-4
7	" "	6	6-1, 5-2, 4-3, 1-6, 2-5, 3-4
8	" "	5	6-2, 5-3, 4-4, 2-6, 3-5
9	" "	4	6-3, 5-4, 3-6, 4-5
10	" "	3	6-4, 5-5, 4-6
11	" "	2	6-5, 5-6
12	" "	1	6-6
		36	

The reader will observe that other than Number Seven, the corresponding small and large numbers go in pairs, according to the number of ways to make them. Thus, Twelve and Two are both made in 1 way; Three and Eleven in 2 ways, etc.

The more thought you give to analyzing these figures, the better you are equipped to play the game. Remember that "prudent man." He "foreseeth" the pitfalls, and turns aside.

Number Seven, with *6 ways* to make it, is the outstanding, all-important figure in the game. It is the frequency with which it turns up that makes the Crap Banks rich. The large majority who put their money down, play the Pass line, the Field, Come, and Six and Eight. The frequency of Sevens here is heavily in favor of the House.

It is that ever-recurring deadly Number Seven that ruins the average Crap player. It is the deadly repetition of Seven that brings forth more cursing, foul language, and displays of anger from those at the table than any other number. One hears so often, "You can't beat this rotten game," "I've no luck," "I've lost two hundred dollars, and I just can't make it come back," and similar remarks.

With this knowledge, one can begin to see that Seven is your enemy . . . or can be *your friend*!

One of the purposes of this study is to reveal some of the friendly gestures that can be made in the case of Seven. It is a number on the Layout that is seldom covered with money. In fact, it is put farther away from the player than any number on the Layout. It does not have the prominent position of Six and Eight, where so much money is lost. For the convenience of the player, Seven should logically be between Six and Eight.

In ancient times, Seven was regarded as the most significant number in life. It represented perfection. Six and Eight came next in importance. If double, they were still more important, and if tripled the meaning was tremendous. All this is true in Craps.

In the Game of Craps, numbers have a very definite value. One should know those numbers sufficiently well to be able to translate that value into dollars.

Your attention is called to the *total sums* of the ways the different numbers can be made.

(7) . . .	6-1	1-6	
	5-2	2-5	
	4-3	3-4	
	15-6	6-15	Total (42)
(8) . . .	6-2	2-6	
	5-3	3-5	
	4-4		
	15-9	5-11	Total (40)
(6) . . .	5-1	1-5	
	4-2	2-4	
	3-3		
	12-6	3-9	Total (30)
(9) . . .	5-4	4-5	
	6-3	3-6	
	11-7	7-11	Total (36)
(5) . . .	4-1	1-4	
	3-2	2-3	
	7-3	3-7	Total (20)
(10) . . .	6-4	4-6	
	5-5		
	11-9	10	Total (30)
(4) . . .	3-1	1-3	
	2 - 2		
	6 - 6		Total (12)
(11) . . .	6-5		
	5-6		
	11-11		Total (22)
(12) . . .	6-6		Total (12)
(2) . . .	1-1		Total (2)

This will be repeated over and over. In any of the usual plays at the Crap Table, the percentages and the odds are all in favor of the House and against the player. There are, however, exceptions where the large odds can be turned in favor of the player—*if* he knows *what to play,* and *when to play,* and *how to play!*

To favor your chance of winning and diminish your chance of losing, know the odds thoroughly.

ODDS OF LOSING (to the House) AGAINST WINNING (for the player)

On Any One Roll

	Actual *Odds*	House *Pays*
No. 7	5 to 1	4 to 1 (made in 6 ways)
6 & 8	6½ to 1	Even money (made in 5 ways)
9 & 5	8 to 1	Even money (made in 4 ways)
10 & 4	11 to 1	Even money (made in 3 ways)
11 & 3	17 to 1	15 to 1 (made in 2 ways)
12 & 2	35 to 1	30 to 1 (made in one way)

The Crap Group (Two, Three, Twelve) 8 to 1, pays 7 to 1.

All *pairs* of the same number called the Hardways, are made in 1 way. The *odds against a particular Hardway turning up in 1 roll is* 35 to 1.

The Hardways		Actual Odds
3-3	4-4	9 to 1
2-2	5-5	7 to 1

In other words, if any Hardways were turning up in a regular way according to the LAW OF AVERAGES, it would appear once in 35 rolls. What are the facts?

The facts are that any given Hardway may not appear in 150 rolls, or it might come the very next roll (infrequent), or just a few rolls from the preceding one.

I have before me records of some 3000 rolls of the dice showing the sum and also the 2 figures that make that sum. You will find that recording a few thousand rolls in a similar manner will be of great value to you. (See page 116.)

Hard Eight (double-Four) shows on the 2nd roll after Eleven. Then again on the 18th roll, and then after 41 rolls, next after 123 rolls.

The first double Five or Ten, the Hardway, shows after 43 rolls, then after 75 more, and not again for 100 rolls.

Hard Six, or double Three, shows on the 99th roll. Again in 66 rolls. Then twice in succession after 7 rolls.

No one can make a profit in playing double Sevens, how much less the Hardways, except as given in *Conclusions.*

On the sheet before me, covering 250 rolls, Number Seven turns up 47 times, an average once every 5½ rolls. A double Seven turns up 6 times in the 250 rolls. The average for double Sevens is close to once in 50 rolls, or once in 7 Sevens. However, a double may appear 6 or 7 times in 50 rolls.

It is very common to see a new shooter throw a dollar to the Dealer to place on a certain Hardway. Often it is done in a "just watch my smoke" manner. Such a bet rarely wins. Many Stickmen urge the players, especially the intoxicated ones, to bet the Hardway. I have never heard any Stickman tell a player to bet Seven. Do you wonder why they suggest the Field and the Hardways to the crowd?

Money placed on the Hardway has 1 chance to win in 35 rolls. It is like reaching for the moon. Even if one has kept a close account of the number of rolls since the last Hardway appeared before he ventures a bet, the odds even then are against winning. However, the Hardways do offer great possibilities.

The rolls of the dice do not give the slightest clue to the appearance of any Hardway. If one has observed that not 1 Hardway has showed in 75 rolls or more, betting all 4 might give results before one was in very heavily. But why not stick to plays that are more conservative?

It is positively uncanny to observe the manner in which the

12 numbers on the dice conform to the LAW OF AVERAGES, in close formation, moving almost like the constellations in relation to one another. Yet, I have a record of 70 rolls between Sevens; 600 rolls between Twelves, and many over 100; 183 rolls between Elevens; 104 rolls between Fours; 50 to 100 rolls between Craps; 120 rolls between Hardways.

On the other hand, in 1 series of rolls, Seven *appeared 35 times in 100 rolls.* In my first 100,000 rolls, Seven *repeated itself 7 times in succession,* and in a few seconds of time. I won the first 2 times (on paper), then I changed to Don't Pass, and was wiped off twice. By that time, I was a little put out, and tossed the dice with a little more vigor, but Seven turned up 3 times. I have made 6 successive throws of Seven several times. In 1 series of 160 rolls, Number Eleven came 22 times.

There was considerable publicity in the newspapers some years ago about a certain movie star making *14 successive* Sevens in a private game. It is doubtful that this could be done in a legitimate public game. The chances are not one in billions.

In many thousands of rolls, Seven averaged 1 in 6½ rolls. In another large series of rolls, double Sevens averaged 1 in 49 rolls, with Seven coming every 6½ rolls, so 2 Sevens should come every 45½ rolls.

But to have *14 successive* Sevens, note these figures:

NO. OF SUCCESSIVE SEVENS		SHOULD AVERAGE EVERY
1	(7)	6½ rolls
2	(7-7)	45½ rolls
3	(7-7-7)	274 rolls
4	(7-7-7-7)	1909 rolls
5	(7-7-7-7-7)	12,410 rolls
6	(7-7-7-7-7-7)	80,665 rolls
7	(7-7-7-7-7-7-7)	524,332 rolls
8	(7-7-7-7-7-7-7-7)	3,408,093 rolls
9	(7-7-7-7-7-7-7-7-7)	22,152,604 rolls
10	(7-7-7-7-7-7-7-7-7-7)	143,991,926 rolls
11	(7-7-7-7-7-7-7-7-7-7-7)	935,957,619 rolls

If you continue computations to 12, 13, 14, or more successive Sevens, numbers go up into the billions. Based upon these figures, the probabilities of the above incident happening are negligible.

In Reno a shill made 8 successive Sevens as I watched the game. One player walked away with $600 won on the Front Line. Note the above table.

9—Rolling the Dice

The one who rolls the dice at the Crap Table is called the shooter. To do so he must have a bet on the Front Line, and any other bets by him are optional.

It is interesting and somewhat illuminating to observe the facial expressions of the crowd lining the table. A few have a happy-go-lucky expression. Perhaps this is their first experience; they're out for a little lark. They may chance ten dollars "just for fun." They see most of the crowd putting their money on the Front Line, so they follow that lead. When a dozen to fifteen are crowding the rail, one has to bet or give way to someone who wishes to lose his money.

One can enter the game in most plays at any time. So the newcomer puts a dollar down, along comes a Crap, and he is out. That may give a sobering thought, but others are there for the fun of it. The next shooter comes along with 2 Sevens and an Eleven, and their spirits soar.

These newcomers have entered the game at a propitious time. It is a winning spell. Instead of losing their $10, they are $20 or $30 to the good. They are now convinced that making money at Craps is a cinch. "How in the world can any Gaming House afford to lose so much money?" They stay on. Suddenly the tide turns. They lose not only their winnings, but the $10 and more, for they feel sure they can make it all back.

The expressions of most people at the table are far from happy-go-lucky. It is a hard, sordid atmosphere, far from that of wholesome living. I have seen men, as they shake the dice violently, and blow on them, and heave them with all their might, reveal the facial expression of a spent marathon runner as he crosses the finish line. I have seen the same strained, contorted faces in a mental hospital. It is not pleasant to see.

It is astonishing to observe the superstitions that prevail among many who frequent the Crap Tables. Some have a definite belief that a magic quality can be imparted to the dice if they are rattled hard, blown upon, rubbed vigorously between the palms, thrown with violence with a snap of the fingers as a final blessing, and encouraged with shouts of the number the player is eager to have turn up. Of course, this is all the sheerest nonsense. It seems especially ridiculous when one observes an apparently educated man going through the same incantations.

Some think the person standing next to him, if not playing, brings bad luck. I had a man swear at me when he saw me just behind him. He picked his money up and walked away.

Superstitions about dice are not limited to the betting public. Many employed in Gaming Clubs, even owners, share in this attitude. Some shills are thought to be especially good in rolling Sevens or Craps, as though they had some mysterious control over the dice.

Let no one deceive you about dice or any control in the roll of the dice—providing of course, the dice are honest. On a Crap Table, it makes no difference how you pick them up, or how you hold them in your fingers. The thrower cannot control the outcome. He might make a guess and hit it, but if he bets on every guess, he will be fortunate to get it once in 6 times.

Dice possess no magic. No one can impart any magic or animation to the dead plastics from which they are made. They are inert, even more so than the ivory from which all dice were made for centuries. Not only do dice lack magic, but no telepathy is going to impart lucky numbers to you by anyone present or absent. I say this, Professor Rhine to the contrary!

Not much ivory is coming out of Africa today, hence the plastics, and they are cheaper. Perhaps if Russia could be persuaded to exhume some of the 20,000,000 mastodons said to be entombed in the frozen mud of Siberia, ivory would appear in dice again. But if they were made right, the story would be exactly the same.

So put it down that the most expert shill or the most expert trickster with dice cannot throw Two, Three, Seven, Eleven, Twelve at will with honest dice, especially with Crap Tables protected as they are today against trick throwing.

The tables are lined with rubber padding, roughened with small diamond-shaped projections which the dice must strike. This is a rule of the House, and the Stickmen enforce it. Naturally, when dice strike this rubber padding, they will rebound in any direction. No one can predict the direction of that rebound or the turn of the dice, any more than one can predict in what direction a frog will jump.

In addition to the many times the dice roll over, and one rolls more than the other, this rebound is to ensure against tricks on the part of experts. Those who bet considerable money have the right to be protected against false dice on the part of gaming clubs.

As a matter of scientific fact, based upon the LAW OF AVERAGES, it does not make a particle of difference whether the dice are tossed twelve feet, or dropped straight down only six inches. The story or outcome will be the same, whether 100 times, or 10,000. Even if the dice make only half a turn, this is so. Any one combination shows the same number of times regardless and notwithstanding. Try it—put down your figures.

Facial expressions often reveal the character. A shooter makes 3 Passes and perhaps a Point or 2. He is hailed as an accomplished dice thrower, or at least a lucky one. Perhaps a heavy bettor throws him a few plunks. Most everyone feels good. *"When fortune smiles, who doesn't?"* The next 4 shooters are out on 1, 2, or 4 rolls. One shoots Two, Twelve, Seven. Scowls are turned on the shooter, some looks of hate; there is *sub rosa* cursing, and some leave the table in disgust—all just as though the shooter had an influence on what turned up. Some shooters are regarded as lucky, and others as being jinxed.

Here is what I turned up in one play: Seven, Three, Twelve, Eleven, Three. How would the crowd like that? Or this one: Four, Two, Nine, Three, Eleven, Twelve, Eleven, Eleven, Eight, Five, Eleven, Seven. Or this one: Seven, Eight, Five, Eleven, Eleven, Eleven, Six, Six, Ten, Five, Six, Six, Five, Five, Two, Six, Five, Five, Four, Four, Five, Seven. Note, no Point is made.

Patience and saying nothing to anyone contributes to one's success. It helps to maintain a calm mind. If your mind is disturbed you are going to overlook numbers, or neglect to put your money down for a final decision and miss it.

Above all, one should not cast angry glances toward a shooter who throws a number adverse to your play. You may do the same for him when your turn comes. For these and other reasons, I never toss the dice in a playing game.

Speaking of the energy some shooters use in throwing the dice, notice how a skilled shill throws the dice. The Stickman slides the dice in front of him, just as to any other shooter—both dice together, and usually as they turned up on the Layout. The shill picks them up with the ends of his fingers and gives them a quick toss so they strike the end of the table with a moderate rebound. He does not shake them, or rub them, or even move them in his fingers. He does not snap his fingers or say a word. In all this, he shows proper sense and good method.

Experienced shills have no more control over the numbers appearing than the typo who throws 27 Passes.

A shill may make 4 to 6 Passes. You say to yourself, "Next time he shoots, I'll bet." He is out on the 3rd roll. You have lost.

However, if he has been preceded by 2 to 4 short plays, he might repeat a former good one.

These are points one should watch carefully to be successful.

10—John Barleycorn and Craps

This combination is a favorable factor to the Gaming Club, but bad for the players. Much money is lost by players because of liquor. It is an outstanding method used by many owners of Gambling Houses to fill their coffers with "unrighteous mammon."

In any Game of Chance, if one hopes to win, or expects to win, he needs all the cleverness his brain can furnish. It takes only a little alcohol to befuddle the mind.

Strange as it may appear, some men entering a Crap Game after a few drinks seem to win more than anyone at the table. I have seen this happen over and over. The reason for this early success is easily explained. Two drinks will overcome the inhibitions of most people. Overcaution and fear, the greatest hindrance to success, are pushed into the background. The lights glitter, the surroundings are cheerful, the world looks rosy. The mild intoxication enables the player, if he knows the game, to place his money with a certain abandonment, and yet with considerable skill. He wins and his winnings pile up before him. He is voluble and delays the game. But the Box-Boss and the Stickmen are patient. They know that if they can keep him at the table he is going to lose it all in course of time. If he is ignorant as well as intoxicated, they advise the Hardways or a Crap. Even the professional Crap player cannot beat John Barleycorn. A rich Crap Club is not afraid of such a player, though he may win for a time.

Although fear and overcaution are removed, more drinks cause the will power to dull and the judgment is affected. It is an unusual man or woman who has had two drinks, who will refuse another, and another, and on to sure intoxication. It is the function of the different bosses on the floor in some Gambling Clubs to see that there are plenty of drinks on hand at winning tables.

When one drinks of his own volition, it is his responsibility. To be offered "drinks on the House" by a very attractive woman who receives a wink from some boss, when a player is intoxicated but winning, is a wicked and reprehensible way of gathering in filthy lucre, very "unrighteous mammon."

In many places, the management sees to it that those winning considerable money have plenty of drinks, if they will accept them. Many times I have seen a Pit-Boss urge a drink on a winning drunken man, stroke his back and tell him he needed a drink to brace him up—a man so befuddled he had practically lost all sense of his surroundings, and could hardly pick up his money.

Anyone winning big money in these places should not take even a drink of water. It is to the credit of quite a few places in Reno and Las Vegas that they do not stoop to such methods.

11—The Game of Rapid Action

When the table is full, no other game is played with the speed of Craps. To keep the cubes rolling as fast as possible is to the advantage of the House. It gives customers very little time to make decisions, and errors in plays are costly to the player. The rapid action also causes considerable confusion.

At times the Dealers are so quick in their manipulations that people barely have time to put their money down.

A possible advantage in being at a crowded table is the fact that at least one person usually is betting considerable money, and the Stickmen give him time to place his bets. These delays enable one to keep a record of the rolls, and to make decisions for the next roll.

In a high-class casino, the noise and rapid action are largely absent. One has more time to make decisions.

A crowded table, with much hilarity in a Gaming House is the one that draws the crowd, for the eager player thinks someone is having a lucky streak. However, the personnel at any table undergoes changes every few minutes. Players migrate from table to table and from Club to Club. Some, believing in luck, walk up quickly to a table, crowd in, place $1 or $5 in the Field, or on Come. If they win, they pick up the money and go to another table. If they lose, they walk away grumbling.

To show how rapid the rolls can be at a Crap Table, I cite from a small notebook the consecutive rolls made at a table in Las Vegas at 7 A. M. There were about six customers and four shills at the table. Some 375 rolls were made in 1½ hours. I have another list of 900 rolls made in 3 hours! I never would have believed this could be done.

In Reno at the Palace Club the pace was terrific at 8 A. M. In one hour I put down 420 figures and then missed a few. Later in the day, at the same table with four or five shills at the table, and the same number of customers, plus one drunk, the pace was close to 500. The bets were small and the Dealers were fast. I had always considered 200 an hour to be fast.

In a total of 1,800 rolls that I put down one day in Las Vegas, Number Seven showed up 519 times, or an average of fewer than *4 rolls* to a Seven. Also Two, Three, Twelve combined gave a total of 333, which is also an unusually high average. The frequency of all these numbers was against the player who followed one or more of the divisions of the game. If one had played *any Crap* only, he would have made a tidy sum. Playing Seven progressively would have given great returns. Were any of these dice off balance? In this series of rapid rolls, the advantage was greatly on the side of the Club.

12—One Million Rolls of the Dice

This series of rolls, covering over five years' hard work, was undertaken with the definite purpose of trying to discover whether there were any loopholes in this popular gambling game as it is conducted at present.

Knowing that no list of figures follows the LAW OF AVERAGES so perfectly as Numbers One to Seven, this study was undertaken to determine, if possible, whether or not any of the 12 numbers made by the 2 dice could be forecast, thus giving certain plays assurance of being not merely a chance.

For the writer, the *final analysis of this extensive experimentation has largely removed the element of chance and "just luck!"* The *conclusions from the Game of Craps is* presented for the reader to determine for himself, whether this is so.

I will explain how these many thousands of rolls were made in order to remove any criticism as to the variety of the rolls and the decisions.

In the first place, several pairs of dice were used, with frequent changes. The dice were given to me by Pit-Bosses of different Clubs in Reno and Las Vegas. The dice had been used on the various tables and discarded after some usage. They were in perfect condition—no rough edges or broken corners.

To give the same results as those obtained on the usual Crap Table, a short runway was built, covered with a smooth cloth and, at the end, was placed a rubber cushion. This cushion was two inches thick, and the surface used was very irregular, similar to the padding on the Crap Tables. The dice rolling against this cushion would rebound most thoroughly.

The two dice were picked up with the ends of the fingers and tossed, or they were shaken in the hands, or rattled in a paper cup. Although this made not a particle of difference in the outcome, it was done to conform to orthodox motions.

As already stated, based upon thousands of rolls and experimenting with various methods, it does not make one iota of difference in the outcome, whether the dice roll over a distance of twelve feet, or you drop them six inches and they make a half-turn. This is so, even if the dice are picked up exactly the same way each time, Seven up, Twelve up, or any number up. I dropped dice six inches onto solid concrete, also with a cloth over it. Both dice will roll, regardless. The croupier does not have the slightest influence over what number will appear, or of knowing what that number will be—*providing the play is honest.*

Dice are fully as inert as a Roulette ball. Those balls are rolled by a machine, and that machine can impart nothing to them except momentum.

In order for one to become thoroughly acquainted with the *rhythm* and *cycles* of dice, and to understand the Law of Averages, the *sina qua non* of the Game of Craps, it is wise to make many thousands of rolls, and to enter the figures in a book for study. Few can achieve success in any endeavor without hard work and careful study. Even in a highly speculative game this is necessary.

It is not necessary to make 100,000 rolls of the dice to know *what they say.* However, you will never regret having done so, because of the impression it makes on your mind of the rhythmic roll of the cubes, and your knowledge of what the next number is most likely to be.

Ten thousand rolls, or even fewer, will give you all the necessary information. But one needs more than information. He needs the greatest possible experience.

It is this constant familiarity with the appearance of the final upturned number, or combination, that gives one "the feel" of what can be expected—what number is likely to appear next, within 1 roll or 3. This can be done so often, that therein lies the profit in the game. (See *Conclusions.*)

It is advisable to roll the dice daily, just to keep in touch with the rhythmic flow of the cubes. One should roll the dice enough so that it will be easy to keep in mind the last 5 or 6 numbers that appear before a Seven. At the table, it is not always convenient to keep a record of the rolls as they appear, but one should both see and hear the number. Playing the uninformed routine way, you do not need to give any attention to this—but how much do you win?

When you have a record before you, at a glance you can take in a dozen figures, and *always the last 3*. Also, you will know *how many rolls have been made.*

This record gives you a better grasp of the game at all times. If certain numbers you are interested in are long overdue, you can tell at a glance. For example, Number Eleven is a very important number in the profitable play of this game. It should appear on an average of *1* in 17 rolls. Suppose your record of figures reveal that Eleven has not shown up in 75 rolls. Would it be safe to "go gunning" for it, remembering it pays 15 to 1? There are times when 2 certain figures together make you believe that Eleven is near, perhaps the next roll. Moreover, if an Eleven has not appeared in 100 rolls, Three or Four may come in the next dozen rolls. If a Crap has not appeared in 75 rolls, how about progressing on "any Crap"?

These are facts you will learn by rolling the dice many thousands of times, so that when certain figures or groups of numbers give you a signal, your mind becomes conscious of it. By lack of attention, one will miss many good plays on the very next roll, plays of which the crowd is totally ignorant. "The simple pass on and are punished."

No one can remember all the features presented in the roll of the dice. Therefore to play a profitable game it is *absolutely necessary* always to have the figures before you to determine your next move. If you are making large bets have someone at your side to keep the rolls before you.

Markings of the Layout

Indicate the Plays that Can be Made

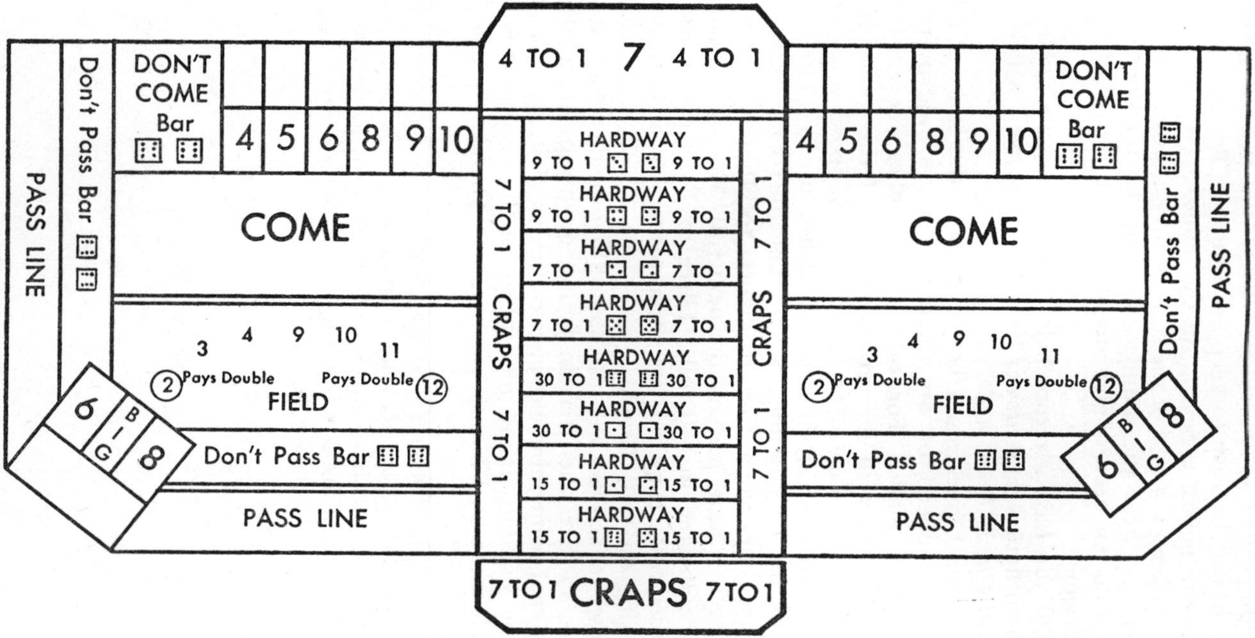

1. *The Front Line and the Point*
2. *The Front Line with Odds*

8. *The Hardways*
9. *Any Crap*

3. *Come Bets and Odds*
4. *The Field*
5. *Six and Eight*
6. *Don't Pass—Don't Come*
7. *Craps*

10. *Craps Two, Three, Twelve*
11. *Eleven. In this book Eleven is treated as a Crap*
12. *Seven, the Outstanding Number of the Twelve, and the Easiest to Forecast*

Place Bets	Place Bets	Place Bets	Place Bets	Place Bets	Place Bets	Place Bets	Place Bets	Place Bets	Place Bets	Place Bets	Place Bets
4	5	6	8	9	10	4	5	6	8	9	10

PASS LINE

COME Ⓒ

DON'T PASS BAR DON'T COME Ⓓ

6 8

Pays Double Pays Triple

② 3 · 4 · 9 · 10 · 11 ⑫

FIELD

PASS LINE

NO CALL BETS ACCEPTED

4 TO 1 7 4 TO 1

9 TO 1 7 TO 1

30 TO 1 30 TO 1

15 TO 1 15 TO 1

ANY CRAPS

7 TO 1 7 TO 1

Ⓒ COME

Ⓓ DON'T COME BAR DON'T PASS

Pays Double Pays Triple

② 3 · 4 · 9 · 10 · 11 ⑫

FIELD

6 8

PASS LINE

NO CALL BETS ACCEPTED

PASS LINE

In checking these various plays in the Crap Game, a careful study of 25,000 rolls has been made, selected at random from different parts of 200,000 rolls. Even 10,000 rolls of the dice will tell all that is to be known, and will furnish as much information as a greater number, owing to the working of the LAW OF AVERAGES. In fact, checking 1,000 rolls may prove whether one given play would be profitable or not.

Those who have developed the Crap Game to its present degree of efficiency (for the House) have displayed all the qualities of a mastermind. However, I have found a few weak spots in the framework. I shall give special attention to these weak spots. (See *Conclusions.*)

Furthermore, there is one point in the game over which the House has no control, and no come-back. That is a "Hot Wind Blowing," namely a shooter who rolls the dice 30 to 50 times before a final decision. This is due to a break in the rhythm. Even one of their own shills may do this. I have counted over 45 rolls by one shill, and he made a large number of Passes—and got a calling-down for it.

In one instance, the "Pit-Boss" removed such a shill during a payoff, and another took his place. The second one went right on rolling up numbers. A change of the dice made no difference. It is during one of these plays that an experienced player can make money very fast. This is a time for progression.

Recently, I witnessed an outstanding demonstration of this point. At 4:30 in the morning, I stepped into a prominent casino. Two tables were still in operation, one crowded, the other with only six shills around it. Fifteen people were crowding the rail of the one table, and many others, making a second row, could not even edge in to place a bet.

I never before saw so much silver on the Layout in front of each player. The money racks were almost empty. The racks were replenished a few minutes after I entered.

Dealers were almost frantic making the many different payments from a few dollars to hundreds. Most of the money was on Pass and Odds, and Come, with piles of silver on every number. A young man at my side reached in between two players and put four $20 bills on Pass. He was given $5 chips. On the next roll he won, and the next one, and the next. I lost track of him because of the excitement.

During a payoff that was consuming considerable time, when everyone's attention was focused on that, I saw the "Box-Boss" remove all the dice from the bowl and slip them into his coat pocket. He replaced them with 5 other pair. Another shooter threw the dice. There was a quick change. Players kept right on putting down large bets. Quite a few left. In ten minutes that table was almost vacated, for the tide had changed. Those who hung on probably lost all they won. However, many did not, for the House lost $4,000 from that "Hot Wind." At Reno, in a very popular Club, a shooter held the dice fifty-eight minutes. The Club lost thousands. In Las Vegas on New Year's, one man rolled the dice for one hour and ten minutes, and the casino lost over $200,000, it was reported.

A few hours later, I talked with the man who did all the shooting. He told me he made 30 Passes. He undoubtedly did not keep accurate tally, but he had made far more than the average. That was an instance when those on Come really went to town.

Here was an instance when a change in dice brought about a change in rhythm. "The prudent man foreseeth the evil and hideth himself; the simple pass on and are punished."

The same day, at a ten-cent Crap Table, a player was on the winning side when a young woman shill took the dice. She made Pass after Pass. The player put down piles of chips on all numbers excepting Six and Eight and the Field. His winnings covered many feet on the rail, and piles on the Layout in front of him. Finally, after some ten or fifteen minutes, the young shill threw a Seven, but the customer must have made close to $100 from ten-cent chips. The "Box-Boss" was angry and took over as Stickman. He hardly gave time to put a bet down. The rhythm changed at once. The large winner lost a considerable amount before he perceived the change and left the table.

However, when you play any one group of numbers, the House has the advantage, excepting when there is a "Hot Wind" shooter. Nevertheless, the disadvantages are fewer than in betting the races.

In Horse Racing, at the very start, the percentage disadvantage against the one who bets is 60%. The favorites win only 40% to 45% of the races. Added to that, you would need to pick the favorite. Even then, if you win 75% to 80% of favorites, and make flat bets, *you lose money*. Regardless of all this, the average attendant at the races would regard the Crap player with raised eyebrows.

PART TWO

13—The Front Line—Pass—The Point

First, last, and all the time it is well to remember that Craps means "to lose." It is well named. When you lose, you are "Crapped out."

The large majority of those who stand at a Crap Table to play put their money on the Pass Line, or Front Line—in many of the places in Reno it is marked Win Line. To a novice that is encouraging, and they follow the suggestion. However, that is a gross deception, for the Pass Line combined with Come bets is a gold mine for the Gaming House. Only the expert can take a profit there—and then only in spots and with sense to quit.

You place your money in front of you and there it remains until a decision. The first roll of a new shooter is called the Come Out. If he throws a Natural, as Seven or Eleven, you win. If he rolls a Crap—Two, Three, Twelve—you lose, you are "wiped out."

If he rolls any other number, as Four, Five, Six, Eight, Nine, or Ten, he makes the Point. The Dealers place a "Marker" on the Point number. If the shooter now makes his Point in the next roll, or on any roll, you win again. *But put it down in your memory, over 50% of all shooters do not make the Point.* Hence, you always lose. If after making the Point, he again throws a Seven or Eleven you win, or if a Crap, you lose.

The Point plays a very important role in making a profit at Craps, hence this statement is made here, but will be enlarged upon in the final section, *Conclusions.* The writer has checked on this fact in over 50,000 rolls and has arrived at some very important factors in winning.

If a Seven comes before the Point is made, all Front Liners lose their money. A new shooter then takes over.

On the Front Line you must win once with each shooter to come out even. You may play one hour and not average 1 win to a shooter. In fifteen minutes you may be ahead 20 units, or you may be out 20 units. You might play any number of hours on the Pass Line and about break even—ahead a little or out a little. This is because of the LAW OF AVERAGES.

It is the *deadly recurrence or frequency of Number Seven* that takes your money. If you want to know *how to beat Seven,* see the last section of the book, *Conclusions.*

If you win 2 or 3 times (with one shooter) on the Front Line, better take your money and wait for the next Come Out. The very large majority of shooters do not make 3 Passes, or even 2 Points. These statements of fact are based upon the checking of 100,000 rolls of the dice.

If you are fortunate enough at the beginning, to have several shooters in succession who roll 10, 15, to 30 to 50 rolls, you may do very handsomely during that period. But be assured a reverse will come. It is bound to do that. Then again I have known a shooter to roll the dice 45 times and not make his Point. You cannot remove your money from the Front Line (and how you wish you could) and so you lose on a final Seven. However, Come bets can be very profitable.

Sevens will cause you to lose more after 2 to 6 rolls than you will win after having 2 successful plays. For, as has been said, you must average 1 win per shooter to come out even.

Here is a friendly tip if you are putting five dollars or more on the Front Line. One hears much cursing from those who walk up to the table and put a ten, a twenty, or even a one-hundred-dollar bill on Pass, and—presto! along comes a Crap (at the Come Out) *and the Stickman* or Dealer rakes in the money. That does not give one a good feeling.

Do this—put one unit on any Crap. It pays 7 to 1. (In this book, a unit means your standard bet; that is, $1 if you are betting dollars, or 10¢ if you are using 10¢ chips. Five units could mean $5, or 50¢.) This protection to your bet is good insurance, as it pays 7 to 1. On $20 you put $3 on any Crap. It does not pay to do this at each Come Out. There may be 30 or 40 Come Outs without a Crap, and then several may show up in quick succession. The average is about 1 to 11 in 13 at the Come Out. Remember, this can also happen after the Point has been made.

Three wins on Pass with 1 shooter is unusual. Your chance of making another win is less than of losing 1 of your winnings by another Seven. However, if you have 3 winnings by 1 shooter, one might just as well "take a chance" for more winnings, and so stay by the play. At times, a shooter may make 5, 6, 8, or even 10 Passes. This feature in Craps is totally unpredictable. As a rule, 8 to 20 shooters will roll the dice before 1 makes 3 or more Passes.

I started to check 10,000 rolls for profit and loss on the Front Line, and recorded every single unit won or lost for each shooter. However, I stopped at 1,600 rolls. This represents four to six hours at a table. Here are the results:

Number of wins 67
Number of losses 154.

This was a cycle when the dice were very "cold," in table parlance, or short plays ending with Seven, and hence very few Points. Only in 75 plays was there 1 Pass, so one breaks even. Only in 4 plays did the shooter make 4 Points.

There were periods when win and lose were about even, or 1 ahead or behind, even 15 to 20, without Points. If one is fortunate enough to get ahead ten dollars at a time like this he'd better quit. One familiar with Craps would not play the Front Line at all at such a time. He would play Don't Pass, or go to another table.

The odds against the Pass, Front Line, or Win Line, in any 1 roll are close to 2 to 1. The chance of winning on the Come Out, after 2 or 3 Don't Pass wins, are quite good. I stood next to a man who put $500 on Pass. He threw 2 Sevens and 1 Eleven. I wanted to tell him to quit, but refrained. He threw a Crap and lost. Then he did quit. That was excellent sense. Also, quick money. The next shooter rolled 4 Craps in succession. The groans and angry expressions! Nearly everyone left the table. Of course, their places were soon taken.

If one is playing Craps for a profit, then the writer does not recommend the Front Line, except in spots. Familiarity with the roll of the dice will reveal about when to look for these spots.

For proof of some of these statements, watch the shills whom the House places at tables as decoys. At dull times of the day there may be six or eight at a table, and no guests. In the best casinos, both men and women are employed as shills. They are nicely dressed, and to all appearances are paying guests. In the cheaper places only men are employed, and many of them look the worse for wear. They are changed very frequently, and usually start with ten or twenty dollars—money furnished by the House.

For years the shills played only Pass or the Front Line. By the dollars in front of them a customer could tell pretty well how the dice were rolling—winning or losing.

It is different today. Quite a few not only play Pass, but also the Field—only one dollar per bet, or one chip, if less than dollars is being bet. The management does everything possible to attract the public to the tables, so no table is left without bettors to roll the dice.

I have never had a shill admit to me that one could make money on the Pass Line; still it is marked Win Line.

But one can take a profit on the Pass Line if he "knows his onions."

One who plays the Front Line can make considerable money with one- and two-dollar bets if Pass and Don't Pass are watched carefully. *Watch the Point always.* If the Point is Six or Eight, your chance of winning your bet is very good. And more times than not you will lose if you put your money on again.

When a shooter is making 15 or more rolls, Pass and Come bets can make a lot of money in a very few minutes. A long series of rolls is more likely than not to be followed by several short plays. Stop at high tide. Wait until there is a rising one again.

When the Pass Line is having a winning period, the reverse is true of Don't Pass—Don't Come. Some discerning bettors alternate from one to the other, after a win. Even this play may seesaw up and down for hours with but little gain or loss—2 wins, 2 losses, 3 wins, 2 or 4 losses.

After some experience with the dice, it is to be observed that some who regularly play Pass combine the play with Come bets, or with Six and Eight Place bets, or even on Six and Eight. These plays can be made very profitable if you know the *when* and the *how*. (See *Conclusions.*)

There is no better way to lose money playing Craps than to play the Pass Line and combine it with Come bets, as the majority of Crap players play the game. As already stated, this is the great gold mine for the House, and the financial cemetery for the player. There is far more money lost here than in any other part of the play. This loss is greatly augmented by playing the Odds at the same time. One may take two hundred dollars with one shooter and lose it all or more with the next. This up and down, seesawing back and forth, can go on for hours.

In fact, the way the average Crap player, with his limited

knowledge, plays the game is like riding up and down in an electric elevator. In a given time just as many ups as downs. The expert can change the ratio, and manage more ups than downs.

14—Come

On the Layout of the Crap Table are long wide spaces marked Come. These spaces are convenient at any part of the table. In fact they are made very prominent, for this is where the House makes most of its money—and the player may make money in spots, or when a "Hot Wind" is blowing.

Tremendous losses are suffered in this play. Most of the money bet on Craps is lost on the Pass Line combined with betting Come, with odds on both.

The House wants the public to make these bets, therefore the spaces are large and convenient. They are not anxious for the public to bet Don't Come and Seven, therefore those spaces are inconspicuous and out of reach of nearly all at the table.

To the right and left of the Pit-Boss, or Box-Man, or in front of the two Dealers, or payoff men, are the numbers Four, Five, Six, Eight, Nine, Ten. When one of these numbers is made by a shooter after you place your bet in the space marked Come, your money is moved to that particular number. This number may be different from the Point made for the Pass Line bettors. The Point is always indicated by a "Marker."

Therefore, do not place your money on Come until the Point has been made. If you place your bet there, it is the same as putting it on Pass. You may remove your money from Come or Pass before the throw has been made, but not after. After your money is in the box, it remains there until your number appears. If so, you win. If a Seven, you lose.

If a Seven or Eleven rolls up while your money is on Come, you win at any time. If a Crap, you lose. Consequently, if you are betting heavily, it is some insurance to place a unit on any Crap. It pays 7 to 1. Crap numbers are quite frequent after the Point has been made.

Come bets offer one of the best possibilities for profit in this game when the Sevens are infrequent. However, no one knows when they will be infrequent, hence the "hazard." But one very familiar with the numbers the dice roll up has some advantage. Periods of long rolls are usually followed by 1, 2, or more short ones. It is several of these short ones that wipe out all the profit on most Come bets.

A little success with Come bets usually starts the player to plunging, making 1 Come bet after another, until he has money in 4 to 6 boxes and odds behind each one. In this instance, if the shooter rolls the dice 20 to 30 times the player makes a killing. He could well afford to take his money and also take a long rest. But he won't. A Seven comes along and he loses all, perhaps the equivalent of 6, 8, or 10 bets. I have checked this play thousands of times and can state positively that in the long run there is no profit in playing the Odds also. A player is better off in making only 1 or 2 at most Come bets at a time, *and no odds.*

There is no greater folly than having stacks of silver on several box numbers at one time. This is reckless gambling. The House is very happy with this type of player. They give him plenty of time to place his money, and they take great pleasure in furnishing him with drinks on the House. They know he will not quit while winning. "The fool and his money are soon parted."

Two Place bets at one time should be the limit. To lose is equivalent to 4 bets, if you also play the Odds. You will lose more times than you will win.

The Come bet is the most difficult method of Crap playing to reduce to scientific rules of procedure. One shooter makes the point in 3 rolls, and throws a Seven, and all Come bets are lost. Another makes 4 rolls and a Seven. The next one perhaps makes 10 rolls. So it goes all day long.

Because of the very careless haphazard way most of the public play, I repeat again, *Come bets are the financial graveyard of the large majority of players, and a gold mine for the House.*

The writer would like to protect you from much of this loss by offering certain *restrictions that will eliminate 50% of the primary loss.* This will give you a far better chance for a profit in the remaining 50% of plays.

In checking 50,000 to 100,000 rolls of the dice, the fact is outstanding that a little over 50% of all plays end in less than 6 rolls. A "play" in this book means the number of rolls between 2 Sevens. Twenty-five percent more of the plays will be under 12 rolls. The remaining 25% covers all plays with 12 rolls and on, mostly under 30, a few in the 40's and 50's.

In 20,000 rolls there were 2,400 plays. With 250 rolls per hour, this would mean standing at a Crap Table eighty consecutive hours.

Twelve hundred of these plays were ended by a Seven in 6 or fewer rolls. That is over 50%. If one had played Come in these 1,200 plays, 6 rolls at least, he would have won 1 bet in 5, or 20%. He would have lost 80%. Where is the profit? It can be seen that in these first 6 rolls the Come bet is seldom won, and if so, the next one is lost—so you break even. If your Come bet is on Six or Eight, the chances of winning are very good.

A very conservative player should let several rolls of the dice pass before he makes a Come bet. If a Seven does not appear under 10 rolls, the rhythm may be broken, and then the Come bets pay off. Better stop with a reasonable profit. Take a rest, or go to another table or even to another Club. Each table has its own rhythm and cycle—for the time being.

15—Don't Pass—Don't Come

These two will be considered as one, for the difference is slight. In Clubs where a difference is made, Don't Come is the better play. In Reno many Clubs put both terms on the same space. When not together, *Don't Come is placed in a corner* out of reach of most of the players. To be sure, a Dealer or payoff man will place your money there if you wish.

For Don't Pass, the player must put his money down before the Come Out. Money can be removed at any time. The Club is very glad to have you remove your money!

For Don't Come, the player need not lay his money until after the Point has been made, or even until any other number has been made. This is an advantage, for one may be especially interested in following certain numbers. It has already been pointed out that next in frequency to Seven, are Six and Eight. So why have your money back of these numbers?

Don't Pass—Don't Come each has advantages, so I play them both. In the long run they balance each other.

Don't Pass has this advantage: Over 50% of shooters never make their Point. So you win your bet. You also win if Crap Two or Three shows up on the 1st roll. Twelve is neutral. The reason Twelve is neutral is because on the whole it appears more frequently, though Two and Twelve should come up the same number of times.

You lose if a Seven or Eleven appears on the Come Out. This occurs quite frequently. With Don't Come this loss can in many instances be avoided. In the long run the Craps will pretty well balance this loss by Seven and Eleven. A Crap is so frequently followed by Seven it is well to wait 2 rolls before entering your money again.

In both these plays, either Crap Twelve or Two is barred. You neither win or lose. As Twelve is so frequently followed by a Seven, I either remove my bet or place one on Seven also. The latter is best.

If a Four, Five, Six, Eight, Nine, or Ten appears, the Dealer places your money (if Don't Come) behind the number showing. This number may be different from the Point made by the Front Line. In that case, if the Point is made you do not lose. You stand a very good chance of winning by a Seven on the next throw. If your number is made before a Seven shows, you lose.

Each of the 6 numbers mentioned can win against a Seven. The 6 numbers are made in 24 ways. A Seven is made in 6 ways, so the odds are 4 to 1 in the player's favor.

As stated, you are at liberty to remove your money at will, and keep your money behind the numbers you prefer.

In this play, do not place your *Don't Pass–Don't Come bets haphazardly.* Most of those who make this play do exactly that. Strangely, this is not one of the popular plays. You see very few making these bets, except occasionally, like throwing a bet down on the Field.

This is the best play on the Crap Table–with certain limitations–as a standard play. You very seldom hear a Stickman urging the crowd to bet the Back Line. They call attention to the Field, to Six and Eight, and the Hardways, and Come.

Before you put your money down for Don't Come bets, have definite numbers in mind you wish to follow. "What numbers?" you ask. To know the most profitable numbers to follow is the very *acme of profit* in making Don't Come bets. (This information is given under *Conclusions.*)

Don't Pass–Don't Come bets should be made in close conjunction with the points in succeeding pages–Conclusions.

It is common practice with most bettors who play Don't Pass, to bet the odds also. In addition, some make large Place bets (other than the Point), gambling with chance that they will make that number before their own is made. Nine times out of 10 this is a losing play, unless the Place bet is on Six and Eight.

It is far safer (at times) to play both Don't Pass and Don't Come, and not put down any odds.

Instead of playing the odds, or several Place bets, there is more profit in watching for indications of a Seven, and putting a few units on that, or doing so progressively. Here again the Field offers many attractive openings, as also do Six and Eight.

16—The Field

The Field numbers are Two, Three, Four, Nine, Ten, Eleven, and Twelve. These Seven numbers can be made in 16 different ways. Most Clubs pay 3 for 1 on either Two or Twelve, or 2 for 1. Clubs differ in this.

Four numbers that come with *devastating regularity* against the Field are Five, Six, Seven, and Eight. These 4 numbers can be made in 20 different ways. So it is clear that the odds are definitely against the player, being close to 2 to 1. So one must beat Mr. Percentage.

In the Field one loses or wins on every roll of the dice. The action is very rapid. When a "Hot Wind is blowing," one may win. However, the way Five, Six, Seven, and Eight repeat over and over in succession is *something deadly*. Think of 9 Sixes and Eights in 12 rolls of the dice! Think of 13 numbers out of 18 taking your money.

Four to 8 consecutive rolls of Five, Six, Seven, and Eight are very common. But with sufficient capital this will not break one. A Field number is sure to come up to break this series of rolls. Seventeen consecutive rolls of these 4 numbers is the longest series I have encountered to date. But 8 to 10 are very frequent.

However, the frequent appearance of Two and Twelve paying 3 to 1, and 2 to 1, compensates for many consecutive rolls of non-Field numbers. After 2 Sevens, a Field number, more often than not, will follow, and particularly so after 3 Sevens.

If one bets every roll of the dice on the Field, the loss is large. Add up the 2 sets of figures in columns (page 55) and note for yourself. In spots of 50 to 100 rolls, one can do very well, as in any other feature of the game.

There are 3 numbers on the Field, which if followed, will permit the bettor to come away with a profit. In fact, one can reduce it to 1 number. In the Field one may avoid many of the Sixes and Eights because they are forecast by a certain number. *Taken all in all, the Field offers the quickest and the greatest profit of all the Crap divisions.* (See *Conclusions.*)

17—Numbers Six and Eight

These numbers on the Layout are large, attractive, and conveniently placed for the public. Putting money on these numbers is a favorite play with no small number of players. Many take "a fling" at them occasionally "just for luck." The House knows definitely that the majority of those who bet these numbers will lose.

In a way the numbers are deceptive. Possibly that is a reason why they are called the "suckers' corner." One standing by or playing the Field, and noting the frequency of Six and Eight, Eight and Six, over and over, gets the idea that Six and Eight must be numbers to win with. So they combine the plays—the Field and Six and Eight. About the time they switch, a lot of Sevens show up in quick succession. They get a jolt, and "Blankety-blank-blank!"

Before you begin betting Six and Eight, you will be well-advised to study the different charts of the consecutive rolls of the dice arranged in columns. You will note every Seven is underscored. By counting the Sixes and Eights, you can easily figure whether you would make a profit if you continued an hour or less or more.

You will observe that very frequently 15 to 40 rolls of the dice will intervene between 2 Sixes or 2 Eights. When there is a lack of one, there will be several of the other. This will indicate that quite a few Sevens have appeared, taking your money if not removed.

Numbers Six and Eight can be profitably played when the Pass Line is winning and when the Come bets are winning. These 3 spots for a win always go together—when a shooter is rolling many numbers between Sevens. One great advantage in this bet is that only a Seven can make these numbers lose. You can let them ride or remove them at will. When you have mastered the indications of an approaching Seven, you can save yourself much loss by removing your money.

Number Seven is made in 6 ways; Six and Eight are each made in 5 ways. Thus together Six and Eight are made in 10 ways against

6 ways for Seven. So *both numbers should be bet.* In 1,000 rolls of the dice, or in 10,000 rolls, Six and Eight will far exceed the number of times that Seven shows up; in fact, almost double the number of times a Seven will come. In other words, Six and Eight, next to Seven, appear the most frequently of all the other numbers. Hence, this can be made a winning play if one knows how to proceed.

Although Six and Eight appear far more times than a Seven, so many other numbers may intervene that a Seven comes along and puts them out of business, and you lose.

If you let your money ride on Six and Eight, there must be 5 numbers between Sevens if you are to show a profit, unless you remove both numbers if *one* wins. In this game it is always wise to bear in mind that over 50% of Sevens appear in 6 rolls. If Six and Eight would alternate in their appearance, the matter would be simple. However, either number may come in flocks, and then not for 20 rolls.

In 500 or 1,000 rolls of the dice Six and Eight will appear in regular rhythm, though in a given 100 rolls there may be quite a difference.

If several Sevens have come in quick succession, then Six and Eight may be played with the possibility of several winnings.

Although it has been said that "the smart player" avoids these numbers as "a sucker's" play, the fact remains that other "smart players" have made thousands on them in a few hours. I have seen hundreds of dollars made on Six and Eight in a very brief time, but not with single dollar bets; rather, ten to twenty dollars on both.

In fact, Six and Eight can be made one of the easiest and quickest ways of taking the coin of the realm from the Layout.

In reality, the expert in understanding the roll of the dice can take a profit from any play on the Layout except the Hardways. Putting money on the Hardways is first, last, and all the time gambling, with the odds greatly against the player.

The actual odds on Six and Eight are 6 to 5, but the House has a 9% advantage because it pays only even money.

There is a sure way to win on Six and Eight. (See *Conclusions.*)

18—The Hardways

These Are:	How Made	No. of Ways Made	Odds	Pays
Hard 4	2-2	1	8 to 1	7 to 1
Hard 10	5-5	1	8 to 1	7 to 1
Hard **6**	3-3	1	10 to 1	9 to 1
Hard 8	4-4	1	10 to 1	9 to 1

The chance of making any one of the Hardways in 1 roll is 35 to 1. Hence, to bet any one of these numbers in a haphazard way is a bad gamble. This play is the most unpredictable of any feature on the Layout. When Six, Eight, Four, or Ten is the Point, it gives the best chance of winning one of these bets. Otherwise a bet is like reaching for the moon.

Any one of the Hardways may come twice in succession, or 5 times in 50 rolls, or not once in 200 rolls. In connection with these Hardways, for the sake of comparison, I am adding double Six, or 6-6, which makes Crap Twelve. This is also made in 1 way, but it pays 30 to 1.

In approximately 2,200 rolls, note the following:

Hard 4 (2-2) came 50 times— 4 is made in 3 ways
Hard 6 (3-3) came 53 times— 6 is made in 5 ways
Hard 8 (4-4) came 48 times— 8 is made in 5 ways
Hard 10 (5-5) came 59 times—10 is made in 3 ways
Crap 12 (6-6) came 53 times—odds 30 to 1.

In another series of 2,700 rolls, note the following:

Hard 4 came 50 times
Hard 6 came 35 times (In one stretch there was an interval of 175 rolls.)
Hard 8 came 28 times
Hard 10 came 45 times
Crap 12 (double Six) came 58 times.

I have not made an estimate of the Hardways on a larger scale than reported here (5000), but I can assume the ratio would be approximately the same if 10,000 or 20,000 rolls were tabulated. With these figures before you, if you were placing money on the

Hardways, you naturally would place it in the order Ten, Six, Four, or Eight. (For later and more extended comment, see page 114.)

You will notice in the series of 2,200 rolls that all Hardways appeared more often than in the 2,700 rolls. In the latter, all Hardways ran closer to the LAW OF AVERAGES.

One outstanding fact established in this tabulation of Hardways in 5,000 rolls is this: Double Six, or Crap Twelve, appears more often than any other double number. So why should any Crap player waste money on the Hardways that pay 7 to 1, or 9 to 1, when Crap Twelve pays 30 to 1?

Moreover, Twelve gives a slight indication when it may be expected. Whereas, the Hardways are absolutely unpredictable within any reasonable time limits. (See *Conclusions.*)

Thus far, in this experimental study, we have considered 8 standard ways of playing the Game of Craps. It is my belief that any 1 of these plays can be made profitable if combined with information given under Conclusions.

The 2 best plays, however, are the Field, Don't Pass—Don't Come, alone or in combination with 2 or 3 methods which the writer has worked out, and knows they will pay a profit regardless of whether the dice are "hot" or "cold."

There are 4 more divisions in this game offered to the public by Crap Banks and Clubs. On these remaining plays the Clubs offer very large odds to the player if he wins, because of the tremendous percentage that is in favor of the House. In these, one must beat Mr. Percentage by observation and progression.

It is very seldom that players systematically bet these numbers, for they are not willing to risk their money against such great odds. *This is because they do not know the game.*

These remaining plays are:

	Odds	Pays
Seven	5 to 1	4 to 1
Any Crap (Two, Three, Twelve)	8 to 1	7 to 1
Two and Twelve	35 to 1	30 to 1
Three and Eleven	17 to 1	15 to 1

These 6 plays—including, with some reservation, the Hardways—*the writer calls them the extremes of the game of Craps. Within these extremes lies the real opportunity to play the game with profit.* This is the Gamblers' Paradise.

For definite reasons, the amazing results revealed by this study of *hundreds of thousands* of rolls of the dice are all included in the final section, Conclusions. These facts and figures are fully copyrighted by the author and no one will be permitted to print or reproduce them in any form.

19—Examples of "Hot Wind Blowing"

7-5-9-12-9-9-9-3-8-8-11-12-10-8-6-3-9-4-10-2-3-9-(**5**)-4-8-6-3-11-10-5-6-3-(**8**)-3-9-11-4-6-8-5-(**9**)-9-10-4-4-2-3-5-4-6-3-(**9**)-9-7.

In these 54 rolls by one shooter the Point was not made until the 23rd roll, and then 3 times afterward. This long stretch was followed by 5 short plays. That compensated for the infrequency of Sevens.

8-9-4-10-6-12-5-10-6-2-5-11-4-3-5-11-4-3-11-(**8**)-6-3-3-5-5-(**6**)-5-4-8-6-(**5**)-5-10-(**5**)-8-4-6-5-6-6-5-6-11-2-10-7.

In the 46 rolls the Point is made only 4 times. (The Point is indicated by the larger bold face numbers.)

In these many hundreds of thousands of rolls, the following is the longest series of rolls between Sevens—65 rolls.
(Just recently 70 rolls between Sevens were made.)

6-(**6**)-6-(**6**)-8-6-10-9-(**8**)-4-(**4**)-9-(**9**)-9-10-6-6-(**9**)-8-9-9-(**8**)-6-5-5-10-9-9-9-4-8-8-9-4-4-5-5-5-5-9-4-3-5-11-9-5-9-4-3-9-11-5-3-3-3-3-(**6**)-6-8-(**6**)-5-8-(**8**)-6-7.

Note that the Point was made 10 times in spite of an interval of 35 rolls between 2 of them.

In a series of rolls as given above, the Front Line-Pass, Six and Eight, Come, and Place bets, and with the Odds, would have paid handsomely. In the last series it began with 6 non-Field numbers, and ended with 8.

This long series of rolls was followed by 5 short plays, 2 to 5 rolls, and no Point. Most players flushed with success would have lost much of their winnings in those short plays.

At Reno a shooter held the dice fifty-eight minutes. A recent report from Las Vegas said a shooter rolled the dice one hour and eight minutes. The casino lost thousands of dollars. This can happen only when a shooter continues to make his Point, followed by Sevens, Eleven and a Crap.

The long series of rolls mentioned above are also examples of broken rhythm. As Seven is made in the most ways, it naturally follows it must appear the greatest number of times. As already stated a Seven should average once in 6½ rolls. While it must be admitted the most extreme irregularities can happen in 1,000,000 rolls of the dice, it is also a fact that the majority—over 50%—of plays are under 7 rolls, when the dice roll according to the LAW OF AVERAGES.

The following are other examples of broken rhythm: (7-12-9-6-8-3-7-11-11-7-11-10-7) (183 rolls between 2 Elevens) (620 rolls between 2 Twelves) (4 Twelves in succession). In 1 series of 350 rolls there were only 27 Sevens, or an average of 1 in 13 rolls. Five Craps in succession, or 63 rolls between 2 Craps (the average is about 11), or 54 single Craps appearing between 2 Craps together. Or 45 plays between two Sevens on the Come Out. Seven is the average. Eighty-seven plays between 2 Elevens on the Come Out; or 15 Sevens in 50 rolls.

It is quite possible that somewhere in 10,000,000 rolls all these figures might be doubled.

The great lesson to bear in mind from this citation is the matter of *progression*. One *must have a definite limit beyond which he will not go*. Take the loss and begin over. In the end you will be ahead.

On a number that pays even money, for instance a certain Field number, it is not wise to progress over 3 times. Even then you only make one dollar, plus the dollars you lost. More will be stated about progression in the final section.

As an example of one way to study the roll of the dice in succession, over 3,000 figures are here arranged in columns. Number Seven is underscored, as it represents the end of the play in most instances. Also, the underscoring makes it stand out clearly, and hence easy to follow. Very much depends upon this Seven. A "P" indicates Pass or the Point. "DP" indicates Don't Pass—Don't Come. In my own records I use a plus (+) a sign for P, and a minus (—) sign for DP. It is quicker. These win and lose signs are very important to bear in mind all through the game.

If a Seven is preceded by P, the shooter has made his Point, and continues to roll the dice. If Seven has DP, it indicates a loss for the Front Line, a win for the Back Line—Don't Pass. Another shooter takes over.

Let 250 rolls represent an hour at the Crap Table—this is a good average if the table is full of players. You cannot win at Craps unless you take plenty of time to study your figures most carefully, counting the Ps and DPs, note the consecutive number of each, note the numbers that precede Seven, and what follow. Make lists and study them carefully.

When you are at the table, always bear in mind the Point. When made, it is of the greatest importance in certain plays. Never forget, when the Point is made, what follows is also of the greatest importance. This will be enlarged upon later.

In the following pages, a number is recorded for each of 3,300 rolls of the dice:

7	4	9	6	5	4	9	6	11+	8+
10	6	8	7-	6	2	10	3	7+	5
6	8	9+	6	6	7-	7-	4	8	6
5	3	7+	8	9	8	9	3	8+	6
7-	8	5	6+	6	7-	6	10	7+	8
10	8	2	8	7-	8	6	5	7+	4
8	6	9	6	8	8+	4	11	5	5+
8	5	4	8+	3	8	7-	5	3	6
7-	4+	7-	7+	3	9	7+	4	3	7-
10	8	7+	6	10	8+	3-	9	4	7+
11	4	4	10	8+	9	6	10	2	4
5	8+	6	9	7+	10	7-	4	11	9
10+	5	10	4	4	4	6	4	10	3
4	5+	4+	7-	3	5	8	10	8	7-
8	7+	8	4	10	10	6+	8	12	8
8	8	4	6	9	10	8	8	9	8+
7-	5	8+	7-	10	9+	5	5	7-	7+
2-	6	9	8	6	4	7-	6+	11+	9
4	7-	10	9	9	5	7+	5	9	4
9	5	3	7-	2	8	8	4	8	7-
3	7-	5	7+	4+	9	7-	8	5	6
9	9	11	6	8	6	4	6	7-	9
11	10	7-	6+	8+	10	4+	9	10	8
7-	4	9	10	6	4+	7+	5+	9	10
8	6	11	7-	3	9	7+	10	5	8
6	6	7-	4	10	4	3-	8	6	4
10	8	8	10	12	6	9	4	11	8
7-	7-	6	7-	9	3	8	6	11	8
6	10	8+	9	8	12	8	5	5	6+
4	7-	8	9+	9	7-	5	6	9	7+
8	6	6	9	8	9	11	12	3	2-
6+	3	5	4	5	4	8	5	10+	9
5	6+	5	5	6+	9+	7-	2	12-	3
5+	9	9	3	12-	4	6	8	8	9+
8	5	5	7-	6	3	11	10+	6	7+
2	2	6	10	9	7-	7-	11+	6	11+
8+	8	10	5	5	12-	8	7+	5	5
8	7-	4	2	9	6	8+	4	3	8
10	9	5	12	5	9	7+	12	3	10
9	6	8+	4	11	7-	10	3	10	10
2	7-	9	5	12	6	10+	11	9	9
7-	2-	5	7-	7-	5	5	4+	8+	10
9	6	3	9	7+	4	2	5	8	6
4	2	7-	7-	8	4	7-	12	7-	5+
7-	5	5	7+	6	7-	7+	6	3-	6

8	11	4	3-	10	4	11+	6	9	6+
4	8	9	6	6	6	8	3	3	2-
8+	5	9	8	5	11	8+	8	7-	8
11+	7-	6	7-	8+	7-	6	12	5	8+
8	9	8	8	7+	8	6+	9	8	5
6	6	6	10	10	3	8	2	11	6
9	6	7-	7-	9	4	6	6	10	6
8+	5	7+	8	6	7-	7-	4	5+	8
5	11	4	12	6	6	7+	10	6	4
9	5	7-	8+	9	8	7+	7-	6+	5+
5+	9+		10	8	4	4		2-	6
7+	12-		7-	11	8	6		8	7-
						7-			

5	4	2-	9	3	7+	7-	10	8	10+
8	6+	6	5	4	9	6	8	3	12-
4	11+	10	9	3	4	11	6	7-	8
7-	3-	4	7-	6+	6	8	9	8	11
6	8	5	5	9	3	8	9	8+	5
4	4	5	7-	7-	3	6+	10	7+	11
6+	7-	6+	7+	8	10	6	4	7+	7-
5	5	6	11+	6	6	11	11	6	4
11	12	7-	9	9	11	5	9	6+	10
5+	8	9	9+	7-	11	6+	5+	7+	5
5	4	7-	6	5	11	6	6	7+	5
6	3	6	8	8	7-	7-	9	10	6
4	8	5	7-	4	8	9	6+	8	9
8	11	6+	7+	2	10	8	6	7-	8
8	7-	7+	8	5+	7-	4	4	6	8
8	7+	10	4	9	8	9+	11	7-	5
5+	8	6	7-	6	6	7+	4	5	7-
10	8+	2	7+	7-	10	7+	4	7-	4
9	6	6	3-	5	10	9	7-	9	3
10+	7-	7-	6	12	6	8	4	6	7-
6	8	4	7-	7-	7-	3	10	2	7+
3	5	3	8	3-	5	4	10	8	9
7-	11	9	10	11+	11	6	8	10	3
6	3	3	5	8	6	10	10	10	3
9	10	12	4	3	6	3	2	8	8
8	4	8	7-	6	7-	7-	10	7-	7-
3	6	4+	3-	6	5	6	7-	5	8
8	7-	5	9	6	7-	9	9	10	11
5	8	4	11	9	9	8	5	6	4
8	7-	6	4	3	7-	2	9+	7-	2
10	4	8	3	4	9	3	5	8	6
7-	7-	11	10	10	7-	4	3	12	9

10	8	7-	8	4	5	8	12	7-	4
10+	12	7+	8	6	12	6+	12	8	6
6	8+	6	7-	6	11	5	6	3	11
11	8	5	6	7-	7-	10	4	5	3
4	6	8	2	6	2-	6	4	8+	9
8	5	9	11	7-	8	7-	9	4	7-
8	6	7-	10	8	10	5	10	5	11+
6+	9	6	9	10	8+	5+	6	11	5
7+	6	4	2	5	6	6	6	7-	4
11+	4	3	10	9	9	8	12	8	10
8	8+	9	7-	8+	3	7-	10	3	2
3	2-	7-	6	7+	7-	5	7-	7-	10
6	6	9	2	8	4	10	10	8	7-
11	4	7-	6+	5	3	6	4	3	7+
7-	5	7+	3-	10	5	9	7-	6	7+
11+	9	6	5	9	8	7-	3-	10	3-
7+	7-	3	3	9	7-	8	12	8+	8
12-	6	8	8	5	10	10	6	6	10
7+	4	10	7-	4	7-	7-	8	5	8
9	8	9	6	11	6	3-	6+	7-	5
9+	5	5	5	9	7-	3-	3-	7+	9
6	11	8	9	6	5	12-	4	10	10
5	9	8	8	10	10	7+	3	3	7-
4	6+	10	10	8+	9	5	9	7	
5	7	7+	8	6+	8	8	7-	4	12
5	2	12-	12	7+	8+	6	7+	10	6
7	11	9	7-	11+	7+	6	11+	6	8
5	7	6	6	6	7+	9	8	4+	4
7	6	9+	6+	5	5	5	11	8	8
4	4	4	7+	10	2	3	12	9	8
9	8	9	12-	5	8	10	8+	3	6
10	6+	6	6	5	5	6	10	9	7-
2	7+	9	8	8	8	9	5	6	7+
8	7+	7-	7-	8	11	8+	11	9	7+
9	10	8	7+	10	8	11+	10+	4	7+
8	7	11	5	8	7	9	7+	7-	8
7	4	8+	8	8	8	6	4	7+	9
9	9	9	4	2	7	2	7-	8	5
9	6	9+	3	9	10	2	10	6	9
5	2	6	8	7-	8	11	10+	3	7-
8	5	10	4	2-	8	10	6	7-	11+
6	8	9	6	7+	10	6	7-	8	8
4	11	6+	5+	7+	5	2	7+	9	5
8	7-	12-	3-	7+	3	7-	9	12	6
7	8	3-	6	9	8	6	6	7-	5

11	9	4	9	3	9	6+	4	6	8+
11	7-	4+	6+	5	6	8	6	5	3-
7	11+	6	7+	3	5	9	9+	4	7+
7	6	10	8	11	7	7-	4	6+	7+
8	5	9	9	6	8	5	10	3-	6
8	5	12	6	4	7	9	10	7+	10
6	5	9	7-	11	11	5+	8	10	3
7	10	10	12-	10	6	8	8	6	6+
6	4	6+	6	5	9	8+	6	9	9
7	12	5	8	11	7	2-	2	3	7-
7	10	10	7-	5	5	5	6	10+	4
12	5	10	11+	11	3	8	2	10	6
5	6+	4	5	3	9	6	8	12	10
6	8	3	7-	5	10	11	6	9	6
11	12	6	6	7-	7	8	3	8	7-
6	10	10	2	7+	2	6	10	7-	4
9	10	4	6+	8	5	3	8	7+	7-
11	8+	7-	7+	5	6	4	8	4	4
9	4	6	6	7-	5	10	4+	7-	11
9	8	4	8	4	6	4	4	4	7-
6	9	9	6+	8	12	3	4+	5	5
5	9	3	6	6	7	5+	7+	10	9
7	7-	9	2	10	11	7+	7+	7-	7-
11	10	6+	6+	7-	6	8	6	8	5
5	6	6	8	8	8	7-	12	5	3
7	9	9	5	12	10	11+	8	6	9
6	7	8	7-	8+	4	9	5	10	9
7	7+	5	8	7+	8	8	9	8+	6
6	11+	4	9	8	2	9+	5	9	9
9	4	3	6	10	9	7+	6+	10	8
3	4+	10	7-	7-	5	7+	10	8	9
7	8	7-	11+	8	10	4	7-	6	8
3	6	9	5	9	6	8	3-	10	7-
4	5	4	7-	5	6	11	10+	8	5
8.	7-	8	6	2	11	8	9	8	7-
7	7+	5	2	8+	7	9	7-	4	
5	5	3	7	5	2	5	9	2	4.
7	6	6	4	4	5	10	9	4	6
7	4	7	6	8	6	4	4	7	7
3	4	6	7	9	4	6	6	6	5
8	9	6	7	7	4	9	3	11	7
2	9	8	8	3	7	7	6	5	6
2	9	4	8	8	7	8	8	9	2
7	5	7	7	7	6	8	5	7	9
8	8	10	3	3	9	9	10	6	12

6	6	7	9	7	6	8	5	8	5
2	7	8	10	8	8	9	8	8	5
3	6	7	6	7	5	7	3	6	8
9	8	4	7	11	6	7	6	9	7
8	10	6	5	7	8	9	6	6	2
3	8	2	3	5	10	9	6	7	6
6	9	7	8	4	7	10	9	8	7
10	10	3	10	11	6	8	3	3	3
6	3	8	6	9	8	9	11	8	6
7	7	5	8	2	8	9	8	10	7
9	12	9	5	2	6	7	12	11	12
5	7	3	7	12	6	7	9	5	9
7	6	5	3	5	2	6	5	10	8
9	6	8	8	2	5	6	4	6	3
6	10	9	7	7	6	3	8	6	9
9	6	8	4	7	7	9	9	6	7
7	5	8	7	7	4	4	4	8	7
5	10	4	8	6	6	6	7	9	9
7	5	6	7	4	7	3	7	2	4
2	9	6	11	12	3	7	8	11	11
8	5	10	7	6	8	8	6	4	6
7	9	9	5	8	8	4	9	7	9
12	9	3	4	6	9	8	6	3	10
9	8	7	11	8	6	8	8	6	7
10	6	11	9	5	8	6	10	2	5
5	5	7	2	3	8	7	11	10	9
6	8	7	2	3	8	7	11	6	7
8	6	7	12	5	6	11	6	7	5
8	8	4	5	2	9	5	10	5	8
8	6	3	2	9	6	7	10	11	9
9	6	7	7	5	6	5	3	5	5
8	8	5	7	5	5	8	9	9	8
8	8	7	7	4	5	8	7	7	9
3	6	9	6	8	8	5	10	9	11
6	7	9	4	9	6	4	6	8	7
3	7	8	12	7	11	7	3	10	9
2	11	8	6	7	8	7	8	5	3
10	5	7	8	5	8	8	8	9	8
6	11	4	6	3	7	7	7	11	6
9	2	6	8	7	7	6	7	8	7
10	8	8	5	7	5	5	4	6	11
9	10	9	3	4	9	9	10	4	7
7	4	5	3	12	8	11	4	7	12
5	9	6	5	9	4	5	11	7	11
7	11	6	7	7	7	10	4	3	10

7	7	7	9	5	6	9	5	4	5
4	11		5	9	5	8	7	3	10
3	9	4	8	5	5	3	5	5	6
8	6	6	5	8	12	8	7	8	7
5	5	9	6	5	8	9	9	7	6
4	3	6	7	12	10	8	6	7	8
3	11	7	12	12	10	11	10	6	8
5	7	7	5	7	8	6	11	11	5
6	9	9	5	6	7	10	9	6	6
10	6	7	7	4	6	6	9	3	5
4	6	9	2	6	8	9	7	8	7
11	4	7	8	6	9	8	5	9	2
2	8	7	5	7	11	10	8	4	2
9	3	7	12	8	6	5	6	5	10
11	9	2	4	9	7	4	8	7	9
8	7	7	10	5	8	12	10	9	10
10	7	7	8	2	6	10	5	7	4
4	5	8	5	9	10	4	7	5	8
8	2	6	5	11	10	2	11	9	4
8	4	2	7	7	6	4	8	7	7
7-	5	6	5	3	4	5	10	7	10
7	3	5	3	8	9	8	10	5	7
11	6	4	3	5	11	10	9	9	6
7	6	9	8	6	9	6	4	9	8
10	4	6	8	4	8	11	4	4	8
4	8	8	5	8	5	10	7	10	10
6	8	10	7	3	3	7	9	6	6
9	12	4	8	3	4	9	6	7	7
7	6	6	6	11	8	10	7	8	9
7	3	9	7	7	9	10	7	8	6
4	10	6	8	3	10	5	6	6	8
5	5	7	7	8	8	10	3	9	3
11	7	9	5	7	8	5	2	7	4
9	7	9	9	8	10	8	6	5	7
8	6	7	6	7	4	8	7	11	10
5	6	11	7	11	5	11	9	3	8
4	7	10	8	9	8	6	11	6	2
8	6	6	11	10	6	6	6	8	5
7	3	10	7	9	6	8	7	4	9
5	10	11	7	6	5	7	9	4	6
9	11	7	6	7	3	10	4	4	7
3	9	10	2	11	9	10	2	7	6
11	12	7	8	8	9	6	8	10	8
5	6	9	7	7	12	7	7	4	8
12	2	9	5	9	6	11	4	7	9

4	6	8	9	5	4	7	4	5	7
8	8	7	6	6	11	9	7	7	8
5	2	3	9	3	6	12	8	10	7
5	6	5	9	11	6	8	3	5	12
5	5	6	6	6	10	6	11	10	7
6	4	6	4	10	7	4	5	6	7
5	9	3	0	10	8	10	8	6	3
4	6	9	4	9	6	12	8	6	11
7	8	9	5	6	7	12	8	10	10
8	8	7	6	7	2	10	5	11	3
7	10	10	10	3	7	10	10	3	7
7	9	6	10	8	7	4	6	6	8
8	6	12	12	8	3	3	7	7	4
8	7	7	5	7	3	8	9	10	6
5	9	9	5	9	7	8	9	8	4
9	7	4	9	6	9	9	12	6	8
5	6	6	2	7	12	12	9	7	8
9	2	7	6	7	8	8	8	5	5
3	6	6	5	7	7	8	6	3	7
9	6	8	7	6	4	10	8	2	5
7	3	3	3	5	10	8	6	4	8
4	10	9	8	10	7	4	9	3	6
8	6	12	3	6	7	9	8	3	5
7	6	7	10	5	8	11	9	10	11
8	8	4	8	6	7	5	4	7	8
8	8	2	6	6	5	5	8	5	8
8	10	4	4	7	7	8	5	9	12
8	5	6	7	10	8	5	5	9	7
2	8	8	6	3	5	9	9	7	
10	7	5	6	8	5	6	6		

20—How to Study the Rolling Dice

In the preceding pages are recorded 3,300 rolls of the dice arranged in columns. The author has similarly recorded hundreds of thousands of rolls of the dice in notebooks. At the Crap Table he uses a small book that can easily be held in the hand and has space for 6 columns of figures. It is obvious that in this way one can see at a glance 200 figures. That is sufficient to enable the player to note the rhythm and the cycle; when the dice "are hot" and when they "are cold," two terms used by the ignorant who do not know how to interpret the rolling dice.

The 3,300 rolls of the dice recorded contain all the facts the author makes use of in the preceding pages and in the final section, Conclusions, to show how one can win in the Game of Craps. *One million* rolls confirm all the points made in these pages, with slight variations here and there in the percentage.

3,300 rolls make 420 plays.*

247 plays were made in six rolls or less, or 58%.

223 plays, *no Point was made,* over 50%.

Those playing Come would have lost in over 50% of bets.

Number Seven came 508 times, average 6½ rolls—very normal. Double Sevens came 78 times, meaning a Seven at the Come Out, averaging one in every seven Sevens, also normal.

Number Eleven came 133 times—average 1 in 25 rolls—normal is 17.

There were many long intervals between Elevens, as 125-137-137 and 183, the longest interval between Elevens in *1,000,000 rolls.*

Any Crap came 327 times—average *1* in *10 rolls.* This would be a wonderful play progressively, if only 10 rolls intervened—however, 60 rolls may roll between 2 Craps. Thirty rolls is common.

Crap Three came 163 times—Eleven came 133 times—both made in 2 ways, so should be about the same. In a greater number of rolls, Eleven is usually slightly ahead.

---

* The number of rolls between 2 Sevens.

Number Six came 395 times—Number Eight came 421 times—both made in 5 ways. Compare these figures with Seven, 508 times.

Pass, winning on the Front Line, came 454 times.

Don't Pass—Don't Come came 483 times.

Occasionally you find 6, 8, or 10 consecutive Passes or Don't Pass, but as a rule it is 1, 2, or 3 of one or the other all day long.

However, the figures given here and more later, show conclusively, Don't Pass—Don't Come is the safer play.

At the table you hear much about betting Eleven after 1 has appeared. As a rule a double Eleven comes about once in 400 to 500 rolls, sometimes 2 doubles are close together.

In the 3,300 rolls, here are the figures—double Eleven came 5 times, 1st in 450 rolls; 2nd in 375 rolls; 3rd in 900 rolls; 4th in 800 rolls, and another in 375 rolls. Only 1 triple Eleven. It is well to remember 3,300 rolls means over thirteen hours at the table, with an average of 250 rolls per hour. From these figures it can be seen that it does not pay to make a 2nd bet on an Eleven. An Eleven comes far more times after Crap Twelve than after another Eleven.

21—Some General Remarks about Craps

No one should feel fully competent to play Craps for a profit until he has rolled the dice at least 20,000 times and entered the figures in a book where they can be studied at leisure. Sevens, Pass, and Don't Pass should be marked in each play.

In fact, before playing at a table, one should always roll the dice in private for a brief period to get the "feel" of the numbers. The more you roll the dice, the easier it is to make quick decisions when you stand at the table.

Your figures will differ very little, if any, from those you see in an actual game. The speed there will be greater, and there will be more noise. One must become accustomed to both of these distractions and not become confused.

In a high-class casino, there is not much confusion or noise or "drunks." The play is not so rapid, and usually there is a more conservative crowd.

Have a definite plan of procedure before you stop at a table. Do not delay to see how the rolls are coming. I have often missed some wonderfully profitable plays by waiting to see whether the numbers were favorable to my plan of operation. *No one knows definitely what the next roll of the dice will be.*

It is an advantage to be at a table where one or two are making much larger bets than the average one-dollar bet. This allows time to put down the numbers as they come and to look them over for preferred play spots. Also to know when 12 or more rolls have been made before a shooter throws out. If he makes 30 rolls, it is well to know it. It is better not to be at an overcrowded table. Four or five shills at a table make no more difference in the roll of the dice than so many customers.

I believe Stickmen and Dealers enjoy seeing the public win, and often try to help them win. After all, it is not their money. By being helpful they make considerable on the side.

At some tables, crowded with a cheaper class of players, the action is so rapid and the Stickmen so noisy with their singsong lingo that the players tire quickly. To play Craps successfully, you must pay undivided attention to the numbers as they turn up. If you find yourself getting tired, take a rest; otherwise, you will make mistakes, neglect good plays, and suffer a setback. If you visit some places in the hours before dawn, you will see men so sleepy and weary at tables they can hardly hold their heads up. Often, they are intoxicated.

The early forenoon hours and after lunch are most favorable for playing a scientific game. The crowd is not there; the Stickmen and Dealers would rather visit than rattle off their usual lingo; the game is more deliberate.

At no time permit yourself to be influenced by the bad advice some Stickmen may be giving to the ignorant or intoxicated players.

There are frequent spots at a Crap Table when nearly any play will give a quick profit. In a different rhythm this may change and be turned into a loss.

There are times when the Front Line, the Field and Don't Pass will seesaw back and forth, a little ahead, then a little behind, but at the end of one or several hours, the player is lucky if he breaks even.

One should have a definite sum to play for, and when that is attained, *stop.* That sum should be moderate, not great and conspicuous. Periods of rest are important, as well as changes of table or Club.

Many Crap players betting the Front Line, or combining it with Come, may win ten to twenty dollars in a few minutes. That is far more than they earn in a day elsewhere. Experience shows it is a part of wisdom to take the money and walk away. Repeat this several times a day. It counts up fast. Otherwise, if one keeps on playing, he will lose it as surely as the sun will come up in the morning.

Note that the majority of players who make considerable sums in an evening will lose it all before morning if they continue playing—usually due to drinking.

Unfavorable groups of numbers are certain to follow favorable ones. When certain numbers *should* appear according to the LAW OF AVERAGES, and another figure shows in its place, this may upset the entire rhythm of numbers, and a shooter goes on and on for a score of 30 or more numbers. Familiarity with the normal roll of the numbers will enable one to hold his bet for the right spot.

The following statement has already been made but it will bear repetition because of a general belief to the contrary: It makes no difference whether you throw and roll the dice twelve feet with all your might—or gently—or merely drop them six inches. Even a quarter of a turn is all that is necessary to reveal the LAW OF AVERAGES.

In playing cards, you are matching your skill and wits against an opponent of perhaps equal skill. In playing with dice in a Game of Craps, you alone possess the skill. The dice do not resist you or play tricks on you. Your skill and knowledge is matched against numbers. *If you do not understand thoroughly the sequence of numbers, you are just gambling,* and trusting to "luck," and make no mistake about that.

Do not start a play you cannot finish. This is particularly important if you make use of progression. Progression can be dangerous. It is well to have a set limit. In the stock market, traders have a "stop-loss order" to save them from a sudden down movement of prices.

If you have an abundance of capital and know how to take advantage of Seven, you are *sure* to win. However, it is bad policy to risk a large amount of money in order to make a few dollars. If you reach the limit in your progression, better take the loss and start over again—and make it up.

Most Crap Banks or Clubs have a set limit to bets posted above the table or on the wall. Many high-class casinos have no set limit. The more big players bet, the more the House makes. It is astonishing to notc how little *experts* know about the roll of the dice.

22—Playing the Odds

Many Crap players with more or less—usually less—experience in the game, with money on the Front Line, or on Come, bet the Odds also. Most players do not know what the odds are, but just the same they put their money down, for they see others doing that.

On the Front Line the Odds payoff is controlled by the Point—Four, Five, Six, Eight, Nine, and Ten, whichever of these appeared on the Come Out, or when the Point is established.

On the Come bets the Odds paid are according to the number your money is placed on. On the Back Line the Odds are according to the number your money is placed behind, but the reverse of Pass.

If your Number is Six, or Eight, the House pays 6 to 5.

If your Number is Five or Nine, the House pays 3 to 2.

If your Number is Four or Ten, the House pays 2 to 1.

On the Come Out, if a natural is thrown—Seven or Eleven—the House pays even money. If a Crap, you lose all.

With your money down on Pass, and on Come numbers, you cannot control the number, and you cannot remove your money. On the Back Line, you can do both.

Playing the Odds is the same as making 2 bets and taking 2 chances in place of one.

Be advised, betting the Odds is not a profitable play, except in spots. A tremendous amount of money is lost in this gamble. Why risk $5 to make an extra dollar, as you must do if your number is Six or Eight. You cannot bet less than $5. You have $10 down, you get back $11—in case you win one bet. If your number is Four or Ten, with a payoff of 2 to 1, and many Passes are being made, then you can afford to take a chance. The money piles up rapidly.

If you do not play the Odds except with Four and Ten, you may do well in spots—when several Passes are made.

Playing the Odds on 3 to 6 Place numbers, an almost universal procedure on the part of players who have some money, is financial suicide—one of the greatest hazards in the Crap Game. If a shooter happens to hold the dice for some time, and rolls them 30 to 50 times without a Seven, then one can make money very fast. *However, it is well to remember always, 50 percent of shooters are out under 7 rolls, and over 50 percent do not make their Point.* So the House or Club gets his money. This statement bears repetition many times.

On the Front Line, with Come and Place bets, a player can take a lot of money in five minutes, but in the next five minutes he can lose it all. Almost without exception this happens. It is rare indeed that a player walks away with a profit.

The author has stood on the "Side Lines" in the casinos in Las Vegas and Reno and watched for hours "big money" play this method (the favorite play with most Crap players) and has seen their money vanish. The day before this page was written, in Las Vegas, a man put down $2000 for chips. He made large Place bets with the Odds. Money seemed to mean nothing to him. Sport was written all over him. He was an old hand. In ten minutes his chips were back in the rack. He bought the same number again. He never was ahead in the play, and left in about fifteen minutes. If he had understood the roll of the dice, and played when the indications were right, he need not have lost.

VERY IMPORTANT

To win at Craps, the Crap player must roll the dice and put down the numbers, until he becomes "number-conscious." This will take weeks and months. A careful study of the following section will save him much time and point out the *winning ways.*

PART THREE

23—*Conclusions*

With Knowledge One Can Win in the Game of Craps

(In the following pages are given the *best* plays and *how to make them.*)

At the very beginning of this final section, I will state that making a profit from Craps is no pushover. It can be achieved only by much hard work, careful attention, and close study—with much practice.

There is no single magical play revealed by the roll of the dice on which you can place your bankroll and say, "I know for certain this will win." There is no such certainty when chance is present. It would be a deception to give any such impression.

Attention is again called to a statement in the Foreword made by an Ohio Judge in a Court of Common Pleas, viz.: "Bridge is a game of skill, not of chance." This is the opinion of a legal mind based on knowledge. Some might disagree with this view.

However, consider the Game of Bridge for a moment. It is played with a deck of fifty-two cards, in which are four suits of thirteen cards, Hearts, Diamonds, Spades, and Clubs. Each suit has the same value, generally speaking. Only four persons can play in a game.

The deck is shuffled and cut and dealt. Assuming the cards are honest, and that the game is honest, it is obvious to anyone that no dealer can possibly know what card he is dealing—nor can the recipient, either, until he turns the card up. *So it is wholly a chance what the card will be.* When all the cards have been dealt, each player holds a totally different set of cards. In a rare instance, once in many millions, or rather billions of games played, all four players can hold a perfect set of cards. This has happened four times in a century, according to recent report.

The Crap shooter who throws the dice in the game is like the Dealer in Bridge—he cannot possibly know what number he will roll, though he can make a pretty good guess. The Bridge Dealer deals thirteen cards. The Crap shooter can make 1 of 11 different combinations of numbers. Up to this point both games are identically Games of Chance. In Craps any number of persons can play the game at one time.

In Bridge each player has to match his wits against three other players who may be equally skillful. At the beginning none of the four can possibly tell what cards the other three hold. He could not possibly *make a guess* what the first play will be. However, from this point on, the game becomes one of skill. But one game will give no clue whatsoever as to what the next one will be.

The skilled Crap player has no one to match wits against except Mr. Percentage. That is one great advantage.

With two guesses, having watched the roll of the dice, he can make a very good forecast of what the Number on the Come Out will be. His forecast will be ten times better than that of a Dealer of cards who tries to tell what four cards he dealt first.

The Bridge player must play the game according to the cards his hand holds.

The Crap player can play any one of half a dozen features of the game. He can play 4 or 5 definite features and win.

So the author takes the position that Craps can also be made a Game of Skill. As in Bridge or Poker, one cannot become skilled overnight.

But be advised that making a profit from Craps, day after day, with its ups and downs, requires definite preknowledge. This point has been emphasized over and over in these pages.

In playing the game scientifically, you may or may not be looking for "spots," and you may or may not be depending on luck. Both can be a help.

The novice may chance upon both of these and make more money than you do for a few minutes, but it is not likely to last long. Do not let this discourage you. It is skill that counts.

The one who has the most knowledge will have the best "luck." Others observing your successful plays will call you lucky.

There are certain prerequisites a Crap player must understand to be successful in the game, as for instance:

1. A rested, calm, undisturbed mind is important. Mental weariness means defeat.
2. A player needs all his wits about him; so no drinking.
3. He must "not be easily provoked." He needs self-control.

4. The best time to play is not when a table is crowded.
5. Duration of play should be less than an hour at one table, unless the player is having exceptional success.
6. The objective should be a reasonable sum. The player should avoid greed.
7. His finances should regulate the amount of his bet, the duration of play, and its objective.
8. He should stop in a winning streak, not in a losing one. But he must avoid plunging—if losing. Stick to your rules. Always be consistent.
9. Pay no attention to "hot" or "cold" dice, except to take advantage of each. Either one may indicate a change in rhythm, or cycle.
10. Pay no attention to the "shooter"—he has no control over the rolling dice.
11. It is best not to roll the dice yourself. It distracts your mind and interrupts your special play.

24—How to Play the Front Line—Pass and Come Bets—for Profit

(A resumé of points already made should be worked out, with added specific information.)

First, last, and all the time it is well to remember that "Craps" means to lose. So when you lose your play, you are "Crapped out," whatever your special play may be. However when you play Numbers Two, Three, and Twelve, you may win.

To understand better the points made in these pages, turn to page 55 and study carefully the summary made on page 62.

The Points made in each of this series of plays are based upon scores of thousands of rolls of the dice, all tabulated.

The large majority of those who stand at a Crap Table to play, put their money on the Front Line or Pass. In many of the gambling places in Reno this line is also marked Win line. To a novice that is encouraging, and he follows the suggestion. However, this is a gross deception, for the Pass Line combined with Come bets is a gold mine for the Gambling House. Only the expert can take a profit there—and then only in spots.

You place your money in front of you and there it remains until a decision. The first roll of a new shooter is called the Come Out. If he throws a natural Seven or Eleven you win. If he rolls a Crap number, Two, Three, or Twelve, you lose.

If he rolls another number as Four, Five, Six, Eight, Nine, Ten, he made the Point. The Dealers place a "Marker" on the Point number. If the shooter now makes his Point in the next roll or any roll, you win again. *But bear it in mind, over 50% of all shooters do not make the Point.* In all such instances, you lose or are "Crapped out" by a Seven. If after making the point, he again throws a Seven or Eleven you win, or if a Crap number, you lose. The facts of the rolling dice show that the Point is frequently followed by a Seven, or Eleven, or a Crap, one of the 3, in about 50% of instances after the Point.

If the Point is made on the 2nd roll, as 6-6, 8-8, 5-5, 9-9, you win. A Seven very frequently follows the making of the Point and you win, or an Eleven, and you win, or a Crap, and you lose. If these 3 numbers do not follow the Point, look out for a Seven on the Second roll, and you lose. This is a very important point to bear in mind if you are betting the Front Line. The writer has checked this fact in over 50,000 rolls and has arrived at some important factors in winning.

If a Seven comes before the Point is made, all Front Liners lose their money. A new shooter takes over.

If you play the Front Line, here is a second fact it is well to remember: Over 50% of all shooters are out under 7 rolls of the dice. Because of these two important facts alone, one may play the Pass Line for hours and just about break even. I have talked with many shills (those who roll the dice for the House) and never has any of them admitted one can make a profit playing the Pass Line if one bets every Come Out for any length of time.

On the Front Line you must win once with every shooter to come out even. You may play an hour and not average one win to a shooter. In fifteen minutes you may be far ahead, say 20 units, or you may be out 20 units, all depending on the rhythm of the rolls, and changing cycles. Over this feature you have no control.

After the Come Out, it is the deadly *recurrence or frequency of Number Seven* that takes your money.

If you win 2 or 3 times (with one shooter) on the Front Line, better take your money and wait for the next indication to bet, or go to another table where the rhythm will be different. The very large majority of all shooters who make their Point do not make a 2nd Point. These statements are based upon checking 100,000 rolls of the dice.

Owing to changing rhythm, in which the rolling dice do not

conform to the LAW OF AVERAGES, as one steps up to a Crap Table, in any given fifteen or twenty minutes, or say, 100 rolls of the dice, the LAW OF AVERAGES seems to have gone out the window. Several (two or three) shooters in succession may roll 10, 20, 30 to 40 rolls of the dice, and you do handsomely if you also play Come bets. *And this is the type of spot to look for* if playing the Front Line. You have made a good winning. Better take your money and stop, or go to another table. Otherwise, you will surely lose it all, for several short plays will follow. (See page 55.)

In this given 100 rolls of the dice there may be 15 or more Sevens, and perhaps several Craps, so you lose play after play. The dice are said "to be cold" (plain rubbish), and everyone leaves the table. In this change of rhythm more Sevens cause you to lose after 2 to 6 rolls than you will win after having 2 successful plays winning on several Passes in succession, and perhaps on Come bets.

Three wins on Pass with one shooter is unusual. Your chance of making another win is less than of losing one of your winnings by "Crapping out" from a Seven. Finally, losing from a Seven is inevitable. However, you can "take a chance" for more Passes, for at times (quite rarely) a shooter does make up to 6 or 8 or 10 Passes.

In a series of hundreds of rolls (see page 55), or a 1,000, or 10,000, a Seven will average 1 to every 6 to 7 rolls, or close to 6½ rolls. This is the reason why about 50% do not make the Point and are out under 7 rolls. This is also the reason why *Come bets are not profitable,* except in *spots* as already mentioned. Then 25% of shooters are out under 12 rolls. With these a few Come bets win.

The remaining 25% of shooters roll from 12 to 50 times. This is the time when the Front Line and Come bets pay off, and how!

Unfortunately for the one with money down, there is no definite order to a few or many rolls. They are all mixed up, as 2 Passes, 1 Don't Pass, 3 Passes, 2 Don't Pass, 1 Pass, 4 Don't Pass, and in this manner the rolling continues around the clock. In time, if you roll and record thousands of rolls, and study these rhythms, you will be able to detect openings for successful playing.

A Seven is made in 6 ways, hence it appears more often than any other number. It also appears more often before and after all other numbers of a Crap series. So a Seven appears more often on the Come Out than any other number. It averages 1 Seven in 7 Sevens. If this average were fixed, Gambling Clubs would have to close their doors.

Two, three, and occasionally four shooters in succession may throw a Seven on the Come Out. If this happens, another Seven may not appear for many rolls, and this is a time to be on the Front Line. As high as 50 decisions by a Seven may occur before another appears on the Come Out.

A Seven on the Come Out means 2 Sevens, when a shooter is out by a Seven. Two Sevens are very frequently followed by Eleven, or a Crap, or both. Let Field players remember this point.

By keeping a record of the rolling dice at the table, one can note when a Seven is long overdue, or by noting, when several are close together, that then one may not appear for many rolls, and so you win on Points and Come bets.

All these facts about Seven might seem on superficial thought to indicate that betting the Front Line was really the Win Line. This would be the case if 50% of plays did not end under 6 or 7 rolls with a Seven.

There are various ways of keeping record at the Crap Table. A small ruled blankbook 3x5 is a very convenient one for putting down the figures—a method the author always uses. Figures may be put in vertical columns, with each Seven decision underscored. Mark Pass with a plus sign, and Don't Pass with a minus sign. With Seven underscored and the two other signs in place, at a glance one can see how the dice are moving.

A second good method is to put the Come Out figures on a horizontal two-line space, with the following rolls under it in vertical columns, with the decision of the play: Pass with a plus sign, and Don't Pass with a minus sign. Note the following pages. At a glance you can see a dozen plays.

Your attention and close study are called to the following 600 rolls of the dice as recorded at various Crap Tables in Las Vegas. In an evening there one can visit some fifty to sixty tables in operation—mostly crowded.

(1)

Come Out	7	11	6	4	10	11	9	6	5	7	5	6	5	9	8	9	8	7	4	8	8	11	7	5
			10	8	5		7	7	3		11	11	3	5	5	7	8		6	11	4			10
			5	6	6				8		10	6	9	7	6				5	6	9			8
			4	9	7				5		9		7		9				4	2	5			7
			8	7							5				11					8	7			
			6												6									
															10									
															12									
															9									
Pass	D-P														7									
	+	+	+	-	-	+	-	-	+		-	-	-	+	-	-	+	+	+	+	-	+	+	-

```
                              (2)
7+
4    Come
8    Out   7 8 7 10 9 3 7 5 3 10 11 9 11 6 7 2 6 9 8 4 4 9 11 4 6 8
7-           9   10 5     5   11          3     10 8 2 5 5 7    8 7 5
7+          11      7         7     4     6      4 3 210 7      8   8
10           7                     10            6 9 8 7       10
4                                   8                           2
10+                                 7                           6
4                                                               3
7-   D-P                                                        7
10         + - +  + - - + + -  -  + -  + + + - + + + - - -  + - + +
3
5                             (3)
7-   Come
7+   Out7 7 6 7 4 8 6 11 5 4 11 11 5 4 11 8 10 10 7 3 6 4 7 3 7  4
11+         6   9 510    7 8       7 7    2 10  7     5 7          6
7+              610 6      4              8           7           11
8               4 5                                                6
4                 2                                                6
2                10                                                6
8+               11                                                2
9                10                                                8
9+                9                                                8
3-                8                                                6
5                                                                  6
8                                                                  9
5+                                                                 5
8                                                                  6
4                                                                  8
8+                                                                10
4                                                                  6
6                                                                 10
6                                                                  8
4+                                                                 6
6                                                                 10
6+   Pass D-P                                                      4
8       + + + + + + +  - + +  + - - + + + -  - + - - - - + - + +
6                             (4)
12   Come
10   Out  11 7 6 12 9 5 10 9 11 2 5 8 11 6 10 5 5 7 8 8 7 4 9 12 6
4            9      9 7  7 5      3 6     4  6 7 8   5 8   811    3
7-           9           6        2 8     9  3   9   5     7 9    7
9            7          12        7      11  7   5   2
11                       7                8          4
2    Pass D-P
7-        + + -  - + -  - - + - - + + +    - + + + + + + - + - -
4
```

(5)

7-
6
9
8
6+
5
8
7-
9
2
7-
9
7-
7+

8
6
8+
6
6+
7+

Come
Out 10 9 10 6 7 7 9 7 6 2 11 8 6 5 8 7 10 9 5 11 12 5 10 8
7 10 6 5 7 6 6 6 6 6 6 5 3 11 10 6
5 9 9 9 10 11 5 9 5 3 4
3 9 7 6 6 5 5 5 8
2 8 6 9 7
2 10 4 8
9 12
6
9
10
11
7

\- + + - + + - + + - + + + + + + - + + + + + + + + + +

(6)

Come
Out 4 8 7 6 4 8 8 5 3 6 3 6 8 8 8 8 10 4 11 3 7 3 12
10 8 9 12 12 7 10 6 3 6 5 8 9 12
3 8 7 5 2 6 3 9 3 8 4
9 2 10 10 8 8 7 10
11 7 7 6
Pass 7+D-P- 7

\- - - - - - - - - + - + + + - + + + + - + - -

(7)

Come
Out 6 10 8 7 8 2 8 6 6 10 5 10 8 11 7 7 7 7 7 7 4 8 4 5 8 6 8 7
6 7 5 8 5 2 4 6 9 10 9 4 7 5 5 8 3 3
6 6 9 4 11 6 3 9 7 9
8 8 7 7 10 11 7 8
7
Pass +D-P-

\+ - + + + - + - - + - + + + + + + + + + + - - + + - + +

(8)

Come
Out 6 7 7 10 6 12 7 4 5 10 6 5 6 7 6 7 6 7 9 7 11 10 12 5 7
4 3 7 6 8 5 8 12 9 4 4 10 9 8
5 5 5 7 4 7 6 9 10 10 6 7 5
6 12 7 5 6 7 7 7 8
6 6 4 7
4 10 4
Pass+D-P- 7 5

\+ + + - - - + - - + - + - + - + - + - + + - - + +

These records of rolls of the dice put down at the Tables are worthy of careful analysis by any Crap player, and particularly one who prefers to play the Pass Line.

Attention is first called to the vertical column to the left. These 60 numbers were made in the Monte Carlo Club in Las Vegas. This is the author's method of recording rolls of the dice for quick appraisement. Pass is marked with a plus sign, and Don't Pass with minus. Decision is underscored, as well as having the plus or minus mark. In these pages a "play" represents the number of rolls between 2 Sevens. A Seven after the point is always Pass.

In the column of rolls the first shooter makes a Pass, a D-P and no Point and 4 rolls. The next shooter makes 2 Passes, so you are 1 unit ahead. One Come bet could have been won, and 1 lost. So that is even. The next shooter rolls the dice 37 times, and makes 11 Passes. Very unusual—about once in 50 to 60 shooters. Twelve to 15 Come bets could have been won. *This is the kind of spot when the Front Line wins, and the only spot.*

Note also one could have won 14 Place bets on Six and Eight. Or big Six and Eight would have won 14 times. So one understanding the rhythms and cycles of the rolling dice can make a clean-up in spots like this one. And, be advised, this is a good time to *stop* with "their money" in your pocket, or go to another table. Long plays like this one are usually preceded by several short ones, and more than likely are followed by a few short ones, and these last can take all your profit. In this particular instance, 6 short plays followed in which no Point was made.

Your attention is called to the approximately 600 rolls of the dice where the Come Out numbers are arranged in horizontal lines as well as Pass and D-P. This method has some advantages.

Note the following analysis of these rolls:

1. 600 rolls of the dice means two to three hours at a table according to type of Club.
2. Number of shooters taking part 63
3. Number of plays under 7 rolls 33
4. Number of plays 12 rolls and over 17
5. Number of shooters making no Point 33
6. Number of shooters making 1 Point 13
7. Number of shooters making 2 Points or more 15
   These 15 shooters made 47 points
8. Number of Points made 60
9. Number of Passes made 109

10. Number of D-P made 75
11. Total units won on Pass Line (net) 54
12. Come bets .... a large loss
13. Number Seven came .... times 98
average close to 6 rolls
14. Number Sevens on the Come Out averaged 1 Seven to 4½ Sevens. The normal is 1 Seven to 7 Sevens.
15. Six and Eight made the Point .... 29 times and lost the Point 16 times.
16. Largest numer of Passes consecutively 10
In this cycle Seven came 6 times, and this happens about once in 100,000 rolls.
Owing to the increased average of Sevens, D-P was not a profitable play.
17. Largest number of consecutive D-P was 6.
18. In these 600 rolls only one shooter rolled the dice 23 times, and another 18 times. For this reason bets on Come were a loss.

The odds against the Front Line—against your winning on any 1 roll of the dice are close to 2 to 1.

Many thousands of tests on a private Layout, and many, many hours of observation at various Crap Tables, giving particular attention to men making five- and ten-dollar bets on Pass and Come, *prove beyond a shadow of a doubt that it does not profit to bet the odds,* except in *spots,* and then in a limited way.

The usual play by the multitude is a *gold mine for the Clubs,* and financial suicide for the player.

As Six and Eight are made in 5 ways, and, next to Seven, appear the most often, these are *outstanding numbers* to bet when playing the Pass Line. *These 2 numbers make their Point more often than any other number.*

A check on thousands of rolls shows that if a player bet a Seven *after every Six on the Come Out making its Point,* he would make a profit. At times a mild progression is necessary. However, though a very sure play, the action is doubtless too limited to suit the average player who is looking for more profit.

With the above points well in mind *HERE IS WHAT THE CONSERVATIVE PLAYER SHOULD DO.*

1. Take time to note the trend of the dice, if inexperienced.
2. Do not bet every Come Out.

3. Wait for three or four shooters to be out on 3 to 6 rolls. Then you may expect one to soon make many more rolls, and may prove to be a spot.
4. However, if at any time Six or Eight is the Point, make a Place bet for those numbers.
5. If your shooter is not out by the 6th roll, begin your Come Bet. A Seven or Eleven may appear and you win. If a Crap, you lose. So if your bet is five units or more, put one on any Crap. That protects your money. Also do the same on Pass Line at the Come Out.
6. If your shooter makes the Point from the 4th to 7th roll a Seven, or Eleven, or a Crap may follow, or all of them in succession. If not and you have money on Pass, place a Come bet, for a Seven very frequently follows on the 2nd roll after making the Point. In this way you break even.
7. If a shooter makes 8 rolls and no decision, the rhythm may be broken, and so a dozen to 50 rolls may follow. So "make hay while the sun shines." Then *stop,* or go to another table, or repeat Number Three.
8. Odds on Six and Eight are 6 to 5. It is wise to bet no Odds on Pass except these two numbers, and then not always. This writer never plays Odds at any time—it is adding risk in a game of chance.
9. To have Odds riding on more than 2 numbers at a time is a great threat to your profit. To have bets in 5 or 6 boxes, and Odds on each one, is plain folly. Only a fool or an out-and-out gambler will engage in such plays. *How the House loves that play!!*

   Only one of these bets can win at a time, but a Seven takes all, equivalent to 10 to 12 bets.

   To be sure, money can pile up fast if the shooter is not out. But the next three or four shooters can lose it all. Watch such plays for a little time and see the money vanish. It absolutely will vanish, for the percentage is against it.

25—*Come Bets*

1. These bets have been touched upon in a previous page, but owing to the multitudes who make this play and lose most of their money, more detail will now be given.
2. The Come spaces are large and made easy to reach from any part of the table. The Clubs wish to make it easy for the public to place their money there. Not so with Seven or some other numbers. Tremendous losses are suffered in this play all day long. On the contrary, tremendous winnings can be made *"in spots,"* when "a Hot Wind is Blowing," and the dice are "hot" (as they say), or in other words when Passes are being made and Sevens are infrequent.
3. Many players place their money in Come spaces as soon as a shooter makes his Point. Your money is placed, in one of these numbers—Four, Five, Six, Eight, Nine, Ten. You cannot remove it.
4. If a Seven or Eleven appears while your money is in Come, you win. If a Crap, you lose. If your number is rolled, you win. If a Seven, you lose all bets with the odds. However, you can remove the odds at will.
5. *Here are the concrete facts to guide one in Come bets:*
   (a) In checking 100,000 rolls of the dice, the fact is outstanding that a little over 50% of all plays *end* in less than 6 rolls of the dice, or say between 6 and 7, for that is the average for Seven.
   (b) In 25% more the rolls will be under 12.
   (c) The remaining 25% covers all plays beyond 12—but a very large majority under 30 rolls. If you could always make your Come bets in this last ¼ of the rolls, you could easily break the bank.
6. In 20,000 there were 2,400 plays, meaning about 80 consecutive hours at the tables. *Twelve hundred* of these plays were ended by a Seven on an average of 6 rolls. This is 50%. If one had played Come bets in these 1200 plays, he would have won 1 bet in 5 or 20%. So he would have lost 80% of his bets. If your money is on Six or Eight, you have a very good chance of winning—at least one bet.
7. At Las Vegas in 1,350 rolls of the dice Come Bets lost 164 times—won 114 times. This meant four or five hours' playing.
8. *Therefore the conservative player* will let several short shoot-

ers be "Crapped out" before making Come bets. Even then he may lose one or two bets before the numbers pile up between Sevens. If a Seven does not appear under 8 rolls, the rhythm may be broken and many rolls follow. It is playing safer not to have down more than 2 Come bets, and no odds.

9. If one can take 50 to 100 units in such a play, and in a few minutes, better be satisfied or go to another table.

26—How to Play the Field for Profit

The Field numbers are Two, Three, Four, Nine, Ten, Eleven, Twelve. These 7 numbers can be made in 16 different ways. Most Clubs pay 3 to 1 or 2 to 1 either on Two or Twelve. Clubs differ on this. In many thousands of rolls Twelve will appear a little more often than Two.

Four numbers that come with *devastating regularity* against the Field are Five, Six, Seven, Eight. These 4 numbers can be made in 20 different ways. So it is clear that the odds are definitely against the player, being close to 2 to 1. Field numbers pay even money excepting the Craps mentioned.

In the Field one wins or loses on every roll of the dice. The action is often very rapid except in the high-class Casinos. When a "Hot Wind Is Blowing" one can play the Field with large profit. However, the way Five, Six, Seven, and Eight repeat over and over in succession is something deadly. Think of 9 Sixes and Eights in 12 rolls! Or 13 out of 18 rolls against you, taking your money.

Four to 8 consecutive rolls of Five, Six, Seven, and Eight are quite common. But with sufficient capital this will not break one. A Field number is sure to break this series of numbers. Nineteen consecutive rolls of these 4 numbers is the longest series I have encountered to date. Sixteen consecutive Field numbers is the longest series of pay numbers. Several Craps were in the list.

So in playing the Field, the frequent appearance of Two and Twelve, paying 3 to 1 and 2 to 1 compensated for many non-Field numbers. After 2 Sevens a Field number, more often than not, will follow, and particularly so after triple Seven, a Crap, or Eleven.

If one bets the Field every roll of the dice, say for thirty minutes, or for any given short period, he may win considerable or he may be much behind. But in several thousand rolls the difference between win or lose would not be great. In spots of 50 to 100 rolls one can do very well, as in any other feature of the game.

With the above points in mind, it is not profitable to bet every roll of the dice, as Mr. Percentage plans on your doing.

There are 3 numbers on the Field Layout, which followed will give the bettor a profit. In fact, one can reduce this to one number to be conservative. One can avoid many Sixes and Eights because they are forecast in very many instances by a certain number. (See *Betting Six and Eight,* page 48.)

Taken all in all, the Field offers the quickest and one of the best plays for profit of all the Crap divisions of the Layout. However, this statement is predicated on following definite rules of procedure, and at all times being on guard against a Seven. To be sure, one will not always win. (See *Outstanding Number Seven.*)

Here Is the Low-down

(a) The safest number in the field to follow with a bet is Nine or Four. They follow each other so often.

(b) After these 2 numbers, is any Crap, Ten or Eleven. A Crap follows a Nine very often.

(c) In 4,500 rolls of the dice Nine and Four were checked. This would mean about 18 hours at a table.

A bet after Nine . . . won 236 times After Four, won . . . 172 times
A bet after Nine . . . lost 155 times. After Four, lost . . . 92 times.
A profit of 161 units.

(d) 3,300 ROLLS were checked for the following numbers: (See pages 55 to 61.)

Bet after Nine won 177 times
Bet after Nine lost 112 times profit 65 units

Bet after Four won 129 times
Bet after Four lost 68 times profit 61 units

Bet after any Crap won 184 times
Bet after any Crap lost 75 times profit 109 units

Bet after Ten won 125 times
Bet after Ten lost 58 times profit 67 units

Bet after Eleven won 93 times
Bet after Eleven lost 34 times profit 59 units.

In the above plays a bet was not made if a Seven was indicated, or units were bet on Seven as a safeguard.

Until you become very familiar with the roll of the dice, it is wise not to bet after any one of Five, Six, Seven, or Eight for a Field number. Watch for a series of 3 to 5 of these numbers to pass before putting your money down. This is about the average before a Field number shows. Bear in mind this is no fixed rule—anything can happen in the roll of the dice.

(e) If Nine, Ten, Eleven precede a Seven, they make a very good Field bet on the Come Out.

(f) Four and Nine are very frequently followed by a Crap, and Crap Three is very frequently followed by Four. Two Fours, Nines, and Tens are quite common. *But after any double, better not bet the Field because Seven is likely to appear.*

(g) Winning on Two and Twelve counts up very fast.

(h) If you bet the field after every Nine only, you will come out ahead in a given time, though there may be 5 to 8 consecutive losses. However, the profit is not large.

(i) If one has plenty of capital, progression on Field numbers after a series of 6 to 10 non-field numbers is not out of order. As a rule, progression on even-money bets is not wise. It can save some losses.

(j) A very definite advantage in playing the Field—one has complete control over his money, so he can remove it at any time.

27—How and When to Play Six and Eight for Profit

"Big Six and Eight" are large and attractive numbers on the Layout, conveniently placed for the public. Putting money on these numbers is a favorite play for a small number of Crap players. Many take a "fling" at these occasionally "just for luck." In a way these numbers are deceptive. Possibly this is the reason they are called "the suckers' corner." One standing by or playing the Field and noting the frequency of Six and Eight, Eight and Six, over and over, gets the idea that Six and Eight must be the numbers to win with.

Six and Eight are each made in 5 ways. While they pay even money, the odds are 6 to 5. The House has an advantage of 9%.

Before anyone bets these numbers for profit, several thousand rolls of the dice should be made, and a close study of the figures made. A close account should be kept at the table. Next to Seven, they appear more often than any other number. Both together appear far more often than Seven.

You will observe that frequently 15 to 40 rolls of the dice intervene between 2 Sixes or 2 Eights. When there is a lack of one, there will be several of the other. This will indicate several Sevens have appeared, taking your money if not removed.

Six and Eight can be profitably played when Pass and Come bets are winning. These 3 divisions of Crap playing for winning or losing go together. Six or Eight can win when a shooter does not make a large number of rolls. If one of these numbers is the Point, you can nearly always win at least once. Bet both numbers.

If you let your money ride on these numbers, there must be 5 numbers at least between Sevens if you are to show a profit, unless you remove both if one of them wins.

Though it has been said the "smart player" avoids these numbers as a "suckers' play," the fact remains that other smart players have made thousands on them in a few hours.

Here Is the Low-Down on Betting Six and Eight for a Profit.

(a) I had recorded over 100,000 rolls of the dice before making a discovery of a number in the Crap game that forecast a Six and Eight.

(b) Then I checked 10,000 rolls of the dice to prove the point. The results were astonishing.

(c) The number that predicts a Six and Eight better than any other number is Number Five.
Number Five is the only number in the Crap game one cannot make a bet on. It only wins on the Point, and in a Come bet.
However, Five in relation to certain other numbers than Six and Eight is exceedingly important. (See *Playing Num-Eleven,* page 97.)

(d) It is almost uncanny the way Six and Eight follow a Five at once or in 2 to 5 rolls. If Five is the Point I do not look for a Five at once. But Six and Eight are pretty sure to appear if a Seven does not roll up.

(e) If a Six or Eight precede a Seven, one or the other is pretty sure to follow in the Come Out.

(f) When a shooter is making many rolls, it is astonishing how frequently a Five is followed by Six or Eight.

(g) In checking 2,000 rolls of the dice:
After Five, Six or Eight followed 105 times.
After Five, Six or Eight lost 77 times.

(h) If Six or Eight is the Point at the Come Out, you are pretty sure of winning 1 or 2 bets–Place bets. They pay 6 to 5. However, be advised, if the Point is made on the 2nd roll, remove your money, and remove your money *after any double*. If a Six appears go back to Six and Eight.

(i) If one bets Six and Eight at each Come Out, he just about breaks even. I checked this point on 10,000 rolls.

(j) When Sevens are coming frequently, stay off Six and Eight, unless they are the Point. Let several short plays pass and then there is likely to be a chance for several winning bets.

(k) To be conservative one can wait until a Five appears before putting money on these numbers, for it is almost a certainty that one of them will appear, even after a Seven.

(l) A definite reason why it is best to bet both numbers is because of the LAW OF AVERAGES. According to this law, both numbers should appear the same number of times, for they both are made in 5 ways.

Note the appearance of Six and Eight in 21,800 rolls:

(6)	Rolls	(8)
1,151	10,500	1,167
127	1,000	126
161	2,000	182
206	2,000	194
230	2,000	214
238	2,300	243
206	2,000	248
2,319		2,374

In a series of 5,000 rolls, Six and Eight came exactly the same number of times.

On the whole I believe Eight has a slight edge on Six.

(m) Here are some figures worthy of study by those who prefer to play Six and Eight.

In a series of 12,000 rolls, there were:

Total number of Come Out	3,815
Total number of Six in the Come Out	501
Total number of Eight in the Come Out	533
Six made the Point	195 times
Eight made the Point	261 times

These figures reveal Six and Eight were in the Come Out one third of the time.

(n) Two persons playing together, one the Field, the other Six and Eight, pooling their results can make a fine showing.

Both should be on the lookout for a Seven. The 2 plays will balance each other, only losing to Five and Seven, when all is considered.

These rules and suggestions are only relative, but they make it possible to play with a profit.

28—How to Play Don't Pass—Don't Come—for Profit

These 2 will be considered as one, for the difference is slight. In Reno many Clubs put both terms on the same line—a great advantage to the player. When not together on the Layout, D-C is placed in a small space on the corner of the Layout out of reach of most of those at the table, but your money will be placed there if you ask for it. The space for these bets on the Layout is far less conspicuous than Pass and Come.

I checked 20,000 rolls to note the relative ratio of Pass and Don't Pass. D-P exceeded P- by 10%. Then I checked 34,000 rolls, P- came 4,100 times. D-P came 4,538 times. In a tabulation of 65,000 rolls, P- occurred 7,553 times, D-P, D-C 9,061 times, or 1,408 times more.

These figures conclusively prove that in the long run D-P is a more profitable play. All Gambling Clubs encourage betting on Pass and Come. As stated before, this is their gold mine.

In checking close to 100,000 rolls of the dice, one discovers the outstanding fact that a little over 50% of all plays end in fewer than 6 rolls. This is one great advantage for playing D-P.

However, in spite of this advantage and these figures, the Crap player must always bear in mind that the Law of Averages does not always roll smoothly. In any 100 rolls of the dice (at the time you step up to the table) almost any departure in the numbers turned up may take place.

On Don't Pass, you must put your money down before the Come Out. Money can be removed at any time. The Club is very glad to have you remove your money.

On Don't Come, you need not put your money down until you

wish to do so. This has its advantage, for you may be interested in following certain numbers.

You lose if Seven or Eleven appears on the Come Out, or after the Point. You win if Two or Three is rolled. Twelve is barred, probably because it appears a little more often than Two. In the long run winning from Craps will almost balance losing from Seven and Eleven. Because Twelve is barred, better remove your bet, for a Seven is more likely to take it than not.

To play for profit consider these points:

(1) More than 50% of new shooters do not make the Point—a definite advantage for this play.
(2) More than 50% do not make a Pass—another advantage.
(3) Number Seven will appear in less than 7 rolls with the majority of shooters. A great advantage.
(4) If your money is behind Four or Ten your chances of winning are better than behind other numbers.
(5) Number Seven averages 1 Seven in 7 Sevens on the Come Out. Watch for this. Bet D-C.
(6) Two Sevens are often followed by Eleven, or a Crap. Note this.
(7) Some shooters will make 30 to 40 rolls. Stay off these bets.
(8) Unless you have plenty of capital it is best not to take a loss from more than 2 Points.
(9) If Six or Eight is the Point, remove your money at once, or place on D-C or make a Six or Eight Place bet.
(10) Make it a rule not to follow D-P more than 4 rolls unless a Seven is indicated. *It is amazing how frequently the Point Nine is made.*
(11) Be sure a Seven does not take your money following the Point. It happens frequently, or an Eleven. Then a Crap.

When you become used to this play, D-P and D-C can be played together. One will balance the other. This way is far better than to bet the odds on the Back Line as most bettors do.

If Ten, Nine, Six, Eight, Five appear on the Come Out and you are playing D-C, it is safer not to put your money down after this first roll due to a Seven coming next roll. However, if the Point is made, then you stand a good chance of winning. So perhaps this suggestion can be ignored. Nevertheless, the observation of these features of the roll of the dice have impressed themselves upon the mind of the author.

The statement is repeated: next to Seven, the frequency of Six and Eight comes next. In betting D-P and D-C these numbers are unfortunate ones in your play unless you make Place bets on them. If you let your D-P or D-C ride on them, even 1 roll, you are pretty sure to lose it within 4 rolls.

Exceptions to removing your money as mentioned are indications of a Seven. It is far more remunerative to place units on Seven when much delayed, and progressively, than betting odds. However, Place bets on Six and Eight may save the day for you.

Be advised, if you bet every Come Out, on D-P you will lose money, for Mr. Percentage is against you.

Here is the Lowdown on the Safest and Surest Way to Win on Don't Pass

(1) Wait for a shooter to throw out after a long series of rolls, 20, 30, or more. Even 12 or 15 may serve the play. More times than not these long plays are followed by 1, 2, or up to 6 or more one to 6-roll plays with no Point. If a shooter is out after 1 roll with a Seven, the *facts show the next shooter will roll a Seven on the Come Out more times than not.* So hold your bet. However, if you do lose your bet in such an event, go right back on.

In this way, you may win often up to 6 or more consecutive plays.

At Las Vegas, following this procedure for a short time at one table, betting D-P after a shooter was out in 2 rolls, here are the results:

No. of times winning	80
No. of times losing	33
Largest No. consecutive wins	10
Largest No. consecutive losses	3
In most instances only one loss	

I have checked on this play sufficiently to know it is the safest way to take a profit from Don't Pass. Your attention is called to the following rolls. These numbers were put down as I stepped up to a table in the Monte Carlo Club in Las Vegas. This vertical column of figures is given on page 75 to prove Pass can win only in spots.

7+	2
4	11
8	7-
7-	4
7+	7-
10	6
4	9
10+	8
4	8
7-	5
10	8
3	7-
5	9
7-	2
7+	7-
11+	9
7+	7-
8	7+
4	8
2	6
8+	8
9	6
9+	6
3-	7-
5	
8	
5+	
8	
4	
8+	
8	
8+	
4	
6	
6	
4+	
6	
6+	
8	
6	
12	
10	
4	
7-	
9	
11	

As stated previously, this is the author's method of recording the dice rolls.

In the long series, *xx,* you will note the shooter made Pass 5 consecutive times. Then one D-P. After that 5 consecutive Passes. This is very unusual. Perhaps not once in 10,000 rolls.

After this long series by one shooter, 5 others follow in quick succession. As the shooter makes 27 rolls without a Seven, naturally several will appear in quick succession according to the LAW OF AVERAGES and to establish the natural rhythm.

Now note the following figures and plays after 2 other long series of rolls:

(1)			(2)			
9	4+	12-	7+	5	10	9
5	9	4	7+	11	11	9
4	7-	5	6	4	7-	3
4	4	8	8	4	9	3
8	9	9	10	11	5	6
8	7-	3	6+	8+	9	8
5	6	6	3-	6	2	5
8	8	6	8	7-	7-	9
9+	7-	7-	4		9	3
4	6		6		7-	9
5	7-				3-	7-
	6				10	
	8				5	
	7-					

Number 1 was preceded by 3 long shooters.
Number 2 was preceded by 2 12-roll shooters.

These short plays after long ones are occurring every few minutes at any table, hour after hour. In time one learns to protect himself when the Point is made.

Number 1 is followed by 7 wins, D-P, and 1 Pass.
Number 2 is followed by 5 D-P, and 1 Pass.

Short plays following a long series of rolls constitute a very regular way of establishing the LAW OF AVERAGES. It is well to bear in mind when a shooter Passes 8 or 10 rolls and no Seven, the rhythm may be said to be broken, and any number of rolls may follow.

(2) There are simple ways of playing D-P to come off with a profit.

(a) Wait until a shooter has made 2 Points, then put your bet down, and watch for indications of a Seven. (See page 91.)

(b) After 2 Sevens play for a Crap or Eleven.

(c) If 2 Craps win on the Come Out, better remove your money, for a Seven or Eleven is common.

How to Play Don't Come

(1) Do not play haphazardly, or be in too great a hurry.
(2) Do not put your money down after any double.
(3) Do not follow Six or Eight at the Come Out.
(4) Also if your bet is placed behind Six or Eight, remove it at once unless a Seven is indicated.
(5) After your money is placed, follow the same rules as given on D-P.
(6) Put your money down after Nine or Four, but not on the Come Out.
(7) A Crap Three frequently follows Four and Nine.
(8) If a Nine follows Four and Five, better wait.
(9) A large bet on D-P or D-C should always be protected against an Eleven. Bet Eleven and do it progressively. (See page 97.) If you have plenty of capital you are sure to win.
(10) There are times when 2 or 3 D-C bets in the same play pay off well.

29—The Outstanding Number Seven

This is the most conspicuous number in the Game of Craps. All others follow in its train, according to the number of ways in which they are made.

Number Seven is the most predictable number in the list of 12. It is obvious, therefore, that Seven is the number to anticipate in the roll of the dice. (See page 55, and Tables 5 and 6, page 92.)

Number Seven follows certain numbers more often than others, and particularly certain combinations of numbers, so that it can be forecast many times in 100 or 1,000 rolls. It can be made profitable to bet it, and it is one of the best bets to be made progressively. At certain times, you can be sufficiently sure a Seven will appear in 1 to 3 rolls that you will win more often than you will lose. This is due to its paying 4 to 1. However, one must know what numbers have preceded it. For this reason, one must keep a record of numbers. If you do not know the last 2 or 3 numbers that preceded a Seven, you may lose out. You will not know what to do on the Come Out.

Next to Seven as a predictable number is Eleven, and after that is any Crap. In all these plays Eleven should be treated as a Crap.

The frequency of Seven has been repeatedly mentioned. One must not forget it.

If Sevens always maintained the rhythm of 1 in 6 to 7 rolls no Gambling Club could stay in business if it was on the Layout. With a reasonable bankroll no one could lose.

The "fly in the ointment" is this: I have a record of 68 and 70 rolls of the dice between 2 Sevens. To progress on that would take a lot of money.

A Seven on the Come Out averages 1 in 7 Sevens, or 1 double Seven in an average of 49 rolls. However, 2, 3 or 4 consecutive Sevens in the Come Out are quite frequent. Three Sevens consecutively average about 1 in 1,000 to 1,500 rolls. Twenty to 30 plays between 2 Sevens on the Come Out is common.

Table No. 5

A TABULATION OF 46,835 ROLLS, WITH 7 AS FOLLOWS

No. of Rolls	No. of Times	AVERAGE	No. of Double 7's
10,000	1597	6¼	220
6000	880	6.8	110
3000	611	5.9	89
3700	535	6.9	80
3800	535	6.9	83
3200	419	7.6	42
2000	337	8.4	
2500	402	6.2	
1000	157	6½	
300	27	13	
100	3	33	
2000	221	9	
135	32	4 plus	
2000	320	6½	
2300	367	6 plus	
2000	331	6 "	

The following table is a tabulation of almost 25,000 rolls to determine the number of times Seven followed Four, Five, Six, Eight, Nine, Ten, and Eleven.

Table No. 6

SERIES OF ROLLS AND NO. OF TIMES OF EACH NUMBER

	3000	3700	3600	10,000	3800	Total No.
7 After 4	33	49	33	76	45	236
7 " 5	30	55	49	140	66	356
7 " 6	55	73	93	200	111	532
7 " 8	55	78	75	208	117	533
7 " 9	42	51	68	204	91	456
7 " 10	39	30	34	158	62	323
7 " 11	45	39	45	120	64	319

This table is a wonderful expression of the LAW OF AVERAGES. Note how closely Six and Eight average up. Nine comes next. Nine and Five are made in the same number of ways but Nine seems to appear more often.

A Check of 10,000 Rolls to Determine the Number of Plays Between Sevens on the Come Out

Number of total plays: 296. Number of plays out of this total from 1 double Seven to the next one, 6 plays or less 226 times. Ten plays or less between, 28 times. Eleven to 15 plays between, 18 times. Number of plays over 15 times, 7. Two Sevens came only once in the following numbers of consecutive plays, 34, 28, 23, 21.

These are figures to bear in mind if you are betting Sevens progressively on the Come Out. This you will do if you follow *Effemar's Master Combination Play.* (See page 103.)

With plenty of capital and no limits placed on bets, one would lose only once in a blue moon, *and then plenty.* For this reason it is well to have a set limit, a "stop-loss" order. (See Table on Progression, page 96.)

Though over 50% of Sevens appear under 7 rolls, there is little or no profit in betting the rolls progressively on each play. *In spots* one can do wonderfully well.

However, one can make a real profit betting Number Seven at the right time, which means following the indications for a Seven. You put units on Seven as you play any part of the game as Pass, Come, Field, Six or Eight, Eleven and any Crap.

30—Indications of a Seven

(1) A Seven follows a Crap number more than any other number. A Seven follows a double Crap (in this I include Eleven) with such regularity it is an outstanding bet for Seven. If the Double Crap is preceded or followed by a Five, it is an even better bet.

(2) Put this down as play number 1 for a Seven. A Seven does not follow every double Crap, so here is a place for a mild progression. Also, following the Crap number or double Crap 1 to 3 rolls pay dividends. Great familiarity with the roll of the dice makes all these bets more profitable.

If a Four or Six appears instead of a Five in the above combination, it is almost as good. In following 3 times, remember a Seven pays 4 to 1, so if you miss 4 times, and win the 5th you are even. What percentage of winning horses pays 4 to 1?

(3) In the tabulated figures Seven follows Three and Eleven more often than it does Two and Twelve. *You will make no mistake*

to bet Seven after every Twelve, and with a mild progression after a loss. Ten consecutive losses is the largest I have had. This is uncommon. The outlay will not strain your capital.

(4) A close study of 25,000 rolls was made to determine if it is profitable to bet Seven after every double, as 4-4, 5-5, 6-6, 8-8, 9-9, 10-10, 11-11. It is noteworthy to see how often a double is followed by Seven, or a Crap number.

The doubles are listed in this order of choice:

1.	6-6	4.	9-9
2.	8-8	5.	5-5
3.	12-12	6.	10-10
		7.	11-11

It seems 4-4 and 5-5 are followed by Eleven or a Crap more often than by Seven.

If one of these doubles is preceded or followed by a Crap, *go after it with* Seven. Do not be afraid to follow it 2, 3, or 4 rolls. After that the rhythm has probably changed.

(5) *Put this down as play Number 2 for a Seven.* This is the outstanding notice of a Coming Seven.

It is true that not every double is followed by Seven, but enough will, so you are on the safe side. Betting every 6-6 on the Come Out will pay a profit, and a good one if progression is used. This has not proved to be true after 8-8.

(6) If a 9-9, or 10-10, are followed by Five, Four, or Six, the Seven will not be far off. In fact, it will not miss very often.

(7) If a triple number (3 times in succession) rolls up as it does on an average once in 275 rolls, as 10-10-10, 9-9-9, 6-6-6, 5-5-5, and a Crap before or after, you can almost "bet your bottom dollar" a Seven will follow in 1 to 3 rolls.

(7) In one series of thousands of rolls, a Seven followed Ten so regularly that it won 3 times out of 4. I thought I had made a real discovery. It proved to be one of those long cycles. In one Club in Nevada, in a series of 1,400 rolls (meaning four to six hours) if every Ten had been followed by a bet on Seven, a fine profit would have been made.

In the same cycle a Crap followed Four so often (nearly always Three) I thought I had discovered a real play. After a short time the cycle changed.

(8) When a shooter is making 20 to 30 rolls, and after a long interval a Ten rolls up, better not forget a Seven. If you lose twice on following Tens raise your bet.

(9) If you bet Seven after every double and after every Ten, you will lose money, and more so if you follow 3 or 4 times. One must be governed by the combination of numbers, and by the trend of the dice.

(10) The reader's attention is called to the columns of figures beginning on pages 55 and 74 in confirmation of the points made here. Note the number of doubles, Craps, Tens, Elevens, Twelves that precede Seven. Note your own rolls—you will have the same results.

(11) In a tabulation of 10,000 rolls, in which there were 1,472 plays, a Seven was indicated by the following numbers:

Nine	preceded	Seven	167	times
Ten	"	Seven	195	"
Eleven	"	Seven	140	"
Doubles	"	Seven	160	"
Craps	"	Seven	197	"

In other words, a Seven was preceded 1.7 times out of every 2 Sevens by one of three numbers. In this estimation Nine, Ten, Eleven were often followed by only 1 roll in less than ⅓ of the times by a Seven.

(12) A third outstanding indication of a near Seven, is an Eleven and a Five, or Five and Eleven, but Eleven, Eleven, Five is even more of a standout. However, this does not come so very often. Eleven, Eleven, Six is almost as good an indication.

(13) A fourth strong indication of a Seven and a safe bet; following making the point, and especially if it is a double. A Seven or a Crap or an Eleven follows making the Point in about ⅓ of all times.

Also a Seven follows on the second roll after the Point is made so often it is a bad bet on Pass, *unless you bet Come or Seven at the same time.*

Checked 10,000 Rolls to Determine: Is it Profitable to Bet Seven on the Come Out?

As stated in former pages, Seven on the Come Out averages once in 7 Sevens or in 50 rolls, or one on an average in 7 plays. In these 10,000 rolls there were 296 plays. So the Sevens on the Come Out are represented by the following figures in parentheses:

(1)- (6) - (11) - (1)- (1)- (1) - (1)- (4)- (1)- (8)- (7) - (5) - (1) -
(1) - (1)- (16)- (10)- (8)- (2) - (1)- (1)- (7) - (1) - (1)- (20) .

The first figure here shows a new shooter rolled a Seven the first roll. Next there were 6 plays before a Seven showed. So you lost

5 progressive bets, and won on the 6th. Ne[illegible]
in which you lost and won on the 11th. No[illegible]
first 15 bets, 14 came in 8 or less on progressi[illegible]
Progression.) That number of progressive w[illegible]
reasonable player.

In these 10,000 rolls there are 3 instan[illegible]
went into considerable money, as 11, 16, a[illegible]
these thousands of rolls would mean you sp[illegible]
tables betting. You could play all day and [illegible]
of losses like this.

One should have a limit for his progressio[illegible]
it. But one with plenty of capital is absolute[illegible]
limits his progression to 20 plays. But be ad[illegible]
wipe out the profit on many winnings.

If "the first crack out of the box" you get
numbers (as 35-28-23), it gives you a chill.

However, the author believes it is better [illegible]
sively, except in spots, and after indications [illegible]
other plays as in *Effemar's Master Combina*[illegible]
one is not out any large amount at any one [illegible]
anced by winnings on other plays.

So with the same amount of capital on[illegible]
money in other plays than just betting 7-7 on[illegible]

Table No. 7

A MILD PROGRESSIVE METHOD FO[illegible]

No. Rolls	Bets-units		Amt. Won	Amt. Lost
1.	2	"	8	2
2.	2	"	8	2
3.	3	"	12	3
4.	5	"	20	5
5.	7	"	28	7
6.	9	"	36	9
7.	12	"	48	12
8.	15	"	60	15
9.	20	"	80	20
10.	25	"	100	25
11.	32	"	128	32
12.	40	"	160	40
13.	50	"	200	50
14.	65	"	260	65
15.	80	"	320	80

A Check of 10,000 Rolls to Determine the Number of Plays Between Sevens on the Come Out

Number of total plays: 296. Number of plays out of this total from 1 double Seven to the next one, 6 plays or less 226 times. Ten plays or less between, 28 times. Eleven to 15 plays between, 18 times. Number of plays over 15 times, 7. Two Sevens came only once in the following numbers of consecutive plays, 34, 28, 23, 21.

These are figures to bear in mind if you are betting Sevens progressively on the Come Out. This you will do if you follow *Effemar's Master Combination Play.* (See page 103.)

With plenty of capital and no limits placed on bets, one would lose only once in a blue moon, *and then plenty.* For this reason it is well to have a set limit, a "stop-loss" order. (See Table on Progression, page 96.)

Though over 50% of Sevens appear under 7 rolls, there is little or no profit in betting the rolls progressively on each play. *In spots* one can do wonderfully well.

However, one can make a real profit betting Number Seven at the right time, which means following the indications for a Seven. You put units on Seven as you play any part of the game as Pass, Come, Field, Six or Eight, Eleven and any Crap.

30—Indications of a Seven

(1) A Seven follows a Crap number more than any other number. A Seven follows a double Crap (in this I include Eleven) with such regularity it is an outstanding bet for Seven. If the Double Crap is preceded or followed by a Five, it is an even better bet.

(2) Put this down as play number 1 for a Seven. A Seven does not follow every double Crap, so here is a place for a mild progression. Also, following the Crap number or double Crap 1 to 3 rolls pay dividends. Great familiarity with the roll of the dice makes all these bets more profitable.

If a Four or Six appears instead of a Five in the above combination, it is almost as good. In following 3 times, remember a Seven pays 4 to 1, so if you miss 4 times, and win the 5th you are even. What percentage of winning horses pays 4 to 1?

(3) In the tabulated figures Seven follows Three and Eleven more often than it does Two and Twelve. *You will make no mistake*

to bet Seven after every Twelve, and with a mild progression after a loss. Ten consecutive losses is the largest I have had. This is uncommon. The outlay will not strain your capital.

(4) A close study of 25,000 rolls was made to determine if it is profitable to bet Seven after every double, as 4-4, 5-5, 6-6, 8-8, 9-9, 10-10, 11-11. It is noteworthy to see how often a double is followed by Seven, or a Crap number.

The doubles are listed in this order of choice:

1.	6-6	4.	9-9
2.	8-8	5.	5-5
3.	12-12	6.	10-10
		7.	11-11

It seems 4-4 and 5-5 are followed by Eleven or a Crap more often than by Seven.

If one of these doubles is preceded or followed by a Crap, *go after it with* Seven. Do not be afraid to follow it 2, 3, or 4 rolls. After that the rhythm has probably changed.

(5) *Put this down as play Number 2 for a Seven.* This is the outstanding notice of a Coming Seven.

It is true that not every double is followed by Seven, but enough will, so you are on the safe side. Betting every 6-6 on the Come Out will pay a profit, and a good one if progression is used. This has not proved to be true after 8-8.

(6) If a 9-9, or 10-10, are followed by Five, Four, or Six, the Seven will not be far off. In fact, it will not miss very often.

(7) If a triple number (3 times in succession) rolls up as it does on an average once in 275 rolls, as 10-10-10, 9-9-9, 6-6-6, 5-5-5, and a Crap before or after, you can almost "bet your bottom dollar" a Seven will follow in 1 to 3 rolls.

(7) In one series of thousands of rolls, a Seven followed Ten so regularly that it won 3 times out of 4. I thought I had made a real discovery. It proved to be one of those long cycles. In one Club in Nevada, in a series of 1,400 rolls (meaning four to six hours) if every Ten had been followed by a bet on Seven, a fine profit would have been made.

In the same cycle a Crap followed Four so often (nearly always Three) I thought I had discovered a real play. After a short time the cycle changed.

(8) When a shooter is making 20 to 30 rolls, and after a long interval a Ten rolls up, better not forget a Seven. If you lose twice on following Tens raise your bet.

(9) If you bet Seven after every double and after every Ten, you will lose money, and more so if you follow 3 or 4 times. One must be governed by the combination of numbers, and by the trend of the dice.

(10) The reader's attention is called to the columns of figures beginning on pages 55 and 74 in confirmation of the points made here. Note the number of doubles, Craps, Tens, Elevens, Twelves that precede Seven. Note your own rolls—you will have the same results.

(11) In a tabulation of 10,000 rolls, in which there were 1,472 plays, a Seven was indicated by the following numbers:

Nine	preceded	Seven......167	times
Ten	"	Seven......195	"
Eleven	"	Seven......140	"
Doubles	"	Seven......160	"
Craps	"	Seven......197	"

In other words, a Seven was preceded 1.7 times out of every 2 Sevens by one of three numbers. In this estimation Nine, Ten, Eleven were often followed by only 1 roll in less than ⅓ of the times by a Seven.

(12) A third outstanding indication of a near Seven, is an Eleven and a Five, or Five and Eleven, but Eleven, Eleven, Five is even more of a standout. However, this does not come so very often. Eleven, Eleven, Six is almost as good an indication.

(13) A fourth strong indication of a Seven and a safe bet; following making the point, and especially if it is a double. A Seven or a Crap or an Eleven follows making the Point in about ⅓ of all times.

Also a Seven follows on the second roll after the Point is made so often it is a bad bet on Pass, *unless you bet Come or Seven at the same time.*

Checked 10,000 Rolls to Determine:
Is it Profitable to Bet Seven on the Come Out?

As stated in former pages, Seven on the Come Out averages once in 7 Sevens or in 50 rolls, or one on an average in 7 plays. In these 10,000 rolls there were 296 plays. So the Sevens on the Come Out are represented by the following figures in parentheses:

(1)- (6) - (11) - (1)- (1)- (1) - (1)- (4)- (1)- (8)- (7) - (5) - (1) -
(1) - (1)- (16)- (10)- (8)- (2) - (1)- (1)- (7) - (1) - (1)- (20) .

The first figure here shows a new shooter rolled a Seven the first roll. Next there were 6 plays before a Seven showed. So you lost

5 progressive bets, and won on the 6th. Next there were 10 plays in which you lost and won on the 11th. Now you will note in the first 15 bets, 14 came in 8 or less on progressive bets. (See Table on Progression.) That number of progressive wins should satisfy any reasonable player.

In these 10,000 rolls there are 3 instances where progression went into considerable money, as 11, 16, and 20 plays. However, these thousands of rolls would mean you spent many days at the tables betting. You could play all day and not encounter a series of losses like this.

One should have a limit for his progression and not depart from it. But one with plenty of capital is absolutely bound to win if he limits his progression to 20 plays. But be advised, 1 such loss can wipe out the profit on many winnings.

If "the first crack out of the box" you get into one of these large numbers (as 35-28-23), it gives you a chill.

However, the author believes it is better to bet Seven progressively, except in spots, and after indications, in combination with other plays as in *Effemar's Master Combination Play.* In this way one is not out any large amount at any one time. Any loss is balanced by winnings on other plays.

So with the same amount of capital one can make far more money in other plays than just betting 7-7 on the Come Out.

Table No. 7

A MILD PROGRESSIVE METHOD FOR PLAYING SEVEN

No. Rolls	Bets-units		Amt. Won	Amt. Lost	Total Gain	Loss
1.	2	"	8	2	8.00	2.00
2.	2	"	8	2	6.00	4.00
3.	3	"	12	3	6.00	7.00
4.	5	"	20	5	13.00	12.00
5.	7	"	28	7	16.00	19.00
6.	9	"	36	9	17.00	28.00
7.	12	"	48	12	20.00	40.00
8.	15	"	60	15	20.00	55.00
9.	20	"	80	20	25.00	75.00
10.	25	"	100	25	25.00	100.00
11.	32	"	128	32	28.00	132.00
12.	40	"	160	40	28.00	172.00
13.	50	"	200	50	28.00	222.00
14.	65	"	260	65	38.00	207.00
15.	80	"	320	80	33.00	367.00

In many thousands of workouts the author has very seldom had more than 20 units on Seven.

Here is a mild progression for playing Seven.

(1) 1-1-1-2-2-2-2, 4, 6-6, 7, 8, 9, 10. Equals 65 units, and 15 selected bets.

(2) 2-2-2, 3-3, 4, 5, 7, 9, 12, 15, 20, 25, 32, 40, 50. Equals 222 units in 16 selected rolls.

It is well not to forget that 15 rolls of the dice are made in a very few minutes. And take it from me, the Club owners are not anxious to have you place money on Seven intelligently. If they were, they would not have Seven out of reach of everyone. I know from experience in Reno and Las Vegas that my persistent placing money on Seven was not welcome to the Box-boss. It makes no difference to the Cashiers, or Dealers.

The best time to bet Seven 2 to 6 rolls is after a shooter has made many rolls, as brought out, betting Don't Pass.

On the contrary, if several Sevens have come in quick succession, one should hesitate on any long progression.

In a progression on Seven, after 6 to 8 rolls and no winner, it is well to skip Six, Eight, Five, and Four, and concentrate on the indications for a Seven. After three Nines, or Tens bet all the rolls that follow, especially Elevens and Craps. You will get your Seven.

INDICATIONS TO BET SEVEN:

1. After 11-5, or 5-11, or 5-11-5. Put a unit on Seven and any Crap.
2. After 5-5 and a Crap before or after.
3. After a Crap, 2 Craps, Five or Four, bet a Seven.
4. After Doubles, with a Five, or a Crap, before or after.
5. After Tens and Nines be alert. Most Sevens appear under 10 rolls.
6. Seven follows the Point more than any other number, on the first or second roll.

31—Playing Number Eleven

Eleven is a very important number in the Game of Craps. As it pays 15 to 1, it is worth while to give some study to it. There are plays in which it can be made very profitable.

Number Eleven and Crap Three pair off together. Each is made in 2 ways. In a check of close to 50,000 rolls, Eleven came 2,169 times, and Three came 2,126 times. Note the consistency in establishing the Law of Averages, only a difference of 43 times.

However, in 500 rolls, or 1,000, one may exceed the other considerably. Strange as it may seem, if 10 Elevens appear in 100 rolls, there may be only 2 or 3 Threes.

Eleven seems to have an affinity for certain numbers, as we noted in other features of the Crap Game.

Following Four, Five, Nine, watch for an Eleven, or after 5-5, 4-4, or 10-10. These last figures are very frequently followed by an Eleven. Particularly is this so if Eleven is long overdue. And the only way you can know if Eleven is long overdue is by keeping a record at the table. The average for an Eleven is 1 roll in 17. Hence, if your record reveals that 60 rolls have passed without an Eleven, it is a pretty safe bet to go gunning for one progressively. The very large majority of Elevens show under 35 rolls.

If an Eleven is followed by a Seven, and the shooter is out, or if an Eleven has appeared in the last 3 rolls, an Eleven often shows on the Come Out. Or it rolls after a Seven, or likely will within 4 rolls.

Other indications of an Eleven:

(a) Watch for one after 7-7 and a Crap.
(b) Following 10-9-10-12—one of the best indications.
(c) Following 5-5, or 4-4 and with a Crap.
(d) 4-5-9, or 5-4-9 is a combination to watch.

Table No. 8

A STUDY OF 25,000 ROLLS OF THE DICE TO DETERMINE WHETHER ANY PARTICULAR NUMBER FORECASTS ELEVEN.

Eleven	followed	after	Four	101 times	= 344 times
Eleven	"	"	Five	119 "	
Eleven	"	"	Nine	124 "	
Eleven	"	"	Ten	80 "	
Eleven	"	"	Seven	197 "	
Eleven	"	"	Six	176 "	
Eleven	"	"	Eight	180 "	
Eleven	"	"	any Crap	123 "	

Numbers Four and Ten are each made in 3 ways. Hence, the number of times should be about the same. However, Eleven does seem to follow Four more often than Ten, and especially 4-4. At times in this survey Ten would be ahead.

Five and Nine are made in 4 ways. It is interesting to note in the 25,000 rolls there is only a difference of 5 times between them. Four and Five together appear 220 times, whereas a Seven rolls 197 times. You will pick more Elevens after Four and Five than you will after Six, Seven, and Eight.

Five or 6 Elevens may appear in 50 rolls, but as a rule, 1 or 2 will show. While the average is 1 in 17 rolls, I have had as high as 180 rolls intervene between 2 Elevens. Once in 10 to 20,000 rolls, 100 rolls or more will intervene. As chance will have it, 2 of these long intervals may come close together. Hence, it is profitable to bet Eleven only under certain conditions.

CHECKED 21,000 ROLLS TO DETERMINE WHETHER IT WOULD BE PROFITABLE TO BET A SEVEN AFTER EVERY ELEVEN.

Eleven appeared a total of 1070 times.

Seven appeared on the	first roll	214	times	} 490
Seven " "	second roll	139	"	}
Seven " "	third roll	137	"	}
Seven " "	fourth roll	84	"	
Seven " "	fifth roll	64	"	
Seven " "	sixth roll	46	"	
Seven " "	seventh roll	42	"	
Seven " "	eighth roll	26	"	
Seven " "	ninth to fifteenth rolls ..	98	"	

Consider these figures:

$3 was bet the first two rolls.
$4 was bet the third roll.
A Seven pays 4-to-1, hence a $3 bet gives $12, a $4 bet, $16.

214 x $12 (if 1st roll won)	$2568
139 x $9 ($12-$3, if 2nd won and 1st lost)	1251
137 x $10 ($16-$6, if 3rd won and 1st and 2nd lost)	1370
Grand total	$5189

In the first 3 rolls Eleven came 490 times.
In the remaining rolls 4 to 15, Eleven came 360 times.
360 x $10 makes $3600; which was lost.
The net difference therefore is $1,589 profit.

In this series of 21,000 rolls of the dice, it proved profitable to bet a Seven after every Eleven for 3 rolls progressively.

But it must be remembered 21,000 rolls means several days at a Crap Table. There were periods when betting Eleven as above proved very profitable, and at other times quite a loss. With plenty of capital it is a pretty sure way of winning. *This is one way of beating the game.*

Eleven on the Come Out averages about 1 in every 4 Elevens. This is well to bear in mind when you are betting D-P. The loss from Eleven is about balanced by wins on Craps.

I checked 43,000 rolls for Eleven on the Come Out. The numbers within parentheses represent the number of plays between Eleven on the Come Out.

(4) (1) (10) (2) (24) (9) (1) (5) (11) (2) (21) (38) (34) (1) (5) (5) (5) (1) (6) (1) (1) [35] (4) (1) (14) (16) (18) (8) (7) (14) (9) (17) (14) (28) (9) (15) (8) (3) (4) (10) (2) (43) (29) (4) (11) (2) (8).

One with plenty of capital, betting Eleven progressively on the Come Out, can make this one of the most profitable plays on the entire Layout. Thirty-five to 40 progressive bets should be the limit.

In the above list of 47 consecutive bets, there is only 1 instance of going over the limit imposed. If one wins 10 to 20 consecutive bets, paying 15 to 1, he should be satisfied, stop, take a rest, or go to another table. I have booked as high as 80 plays between Elevens. One loss of 40 bets can consume the profit of many wins. The big gambler with a "wad of money" can surely "go to town" on this play. He should have some one keep score for him.

If one wins several times on short plays, to avoid a possible long stretch without a winner, he can pass 6, 10, 15, or 20 plays before betting again.

Personally, I do not do this because I make up any loss on progressive bets by winning on the Field, D-P, Six and Eight Place bets, or on any Crap. For this see *Effemar's Master Combination Play,* page 103.

If you roll the dice a few thousand times for your own profit, you will note that Eleven very frequently follows making the Point. If you are betting Pass this is to your advantage, but against you if on D-P. This is a good time to place a unit on Eleven.

METHOD FOR PROGRESSION BETTING ON ELEVEN

1.	Bet 2 units	10 times	equals	20 units
2.	Bet 3 units	5 times	"	15 units
3.	Bet 4 units	3 times	"	12 units
4.	Bet 5 units	3 times	"	15 units
5.	Bet 7 units	5 times	"	35 units
6.	Bet 9 units	4 times	"	36 units
	TOTAL BETS—30			133 units

You should memorize these figures, or have them before you. One with large capital can double or triple these figures in the same ratio. You certainly "go to town" in this play. One with small capital can begin with half the amount of the above bets. Or even with ten-cent chips, the profit can mount up very rapidly.

In the author's opinion, for a progression bet on any feature of the game, this is one of the best and the surest of profit. It is just the same all the time whether the "dice are hot or cold."

Unless one is winning continuously and is far ahead with "his money," it is not to his profit to remain at one table very long.

32—Betting the Crap Numbers Two, Three, and Twelve

Number Three is made the same number of ways as Eleven, so as already shown they appear about the same number of times in any given number of rolls. However, although Three is not as predictable as Eleven, all that has been written about betting Eleven in the Come Out will apply to Three also, and both pay 15 to 1.

Two and Twelve are unpredictable. But strange as it may seem, 2 of 1 or 1 of each appear close together, often within 6 rolls. Or they frequently follow Three or Eleven. I have rolled 4 Twelves in succession, also 4 Elevens and 4 Threes. Including Eleven, I have rolled 7 of these numbers in a row.

On the average a Crap appears once in 10 or 11 rolls, although from 50 to 100 rolls may intervene between any 2 Craps. I have had over 600 rolls intervene between 2 Twelves. If Eleven is included with the Craps, it is very seldom that 50 rolls will intervene between these 4 numbers.

There are periods of one to several hundred rolls when one can make a fine profit betting any Crap every roll with a progression to 3 units. It pays 7 to 1.

Number Three follows Four, Six, Seven, and Eight more than any other numbers. Nine comes next. There are cycles when a Three follows Four so regularly or within 4 rolls that it is a pretty safe bet to place. This is particularly true if one is long overdue. In passing this is a good point for Field betting.

Number Eleven follows Three far more often than it does Twelve. If one bets any Crap he should put a unit on Eleven.

If a Crap is long overdue, which one can tell in a moment if he has kept a record, one may "go fishing" for it. In that case put a unit on Two, Three, Eleven, Twelve, and 2 on Seven. By having 2 on Seven you will very often save, and make 4 units if the Crap is lost. This will save many a bet that otherwise is lost—for Craps and Seven go close together.

The closest approach to forecasting a Crap is on the 1st or 2nd roll after 1 has appeared. Particularly is this true if 1 has appeared 1 to 3 rolls before the last Seven. In this case a Crap very frequently appears on the Come Out. A Crap follows a Seven or Eleven more times than any other number. And a Crap frequently follows a Nine or Four.

A double Crap will average about once every 7 Craps. Two may be close together, and then not 1 for 200 or 300 rolls. For this reason it is not profitable to bet 2 Craps progressively. I checked this play for 30,000 rolls. There are periods when one can take considerable profit.

Table No. 9

TABLE OF PROGRESSIVE BETS ON CRAPS, ELEVEN, and SEVEN

NO. BETS	BETS ON 7-CRAPS-11		TOTAL BETS		WIN		LOSE
1.	2---4		6	units	(5-10-25)	units	6
2.	2---4		6	"	(5-10-25)	"	12
3.	3---4		7	"	(8-10-25)	"	19
4.	4---4		8	"	(12-25-25)	"	27
5.	5---6	(2 on 3-11)	11	"	(13-25-25)	"	38
6.	6---6	(" " " ")	12	"	(18-25-25)	"	50
7.	7---8-4	(4 on 3-11)	19	"	(16-45-45)	"	71
8.	8---8-4		20	"	(20-34-32)	"	93
9.	8---6-8		22	"	(16-54-69)	"	117
10.	10--12-6		28	"	(28-66-66)	"	145
11.	14--14-8		36	"	(30-79-88)	"	181
12.	16--14-8		38	"	(42-79-88)	"	219

In this progression each time a unit is added to Two and Twelve, 2 units are added to Three and Eleven.

In all these bets the one placed on Seven is for the purpose of taking care of losses on the other figures

Checking 10,000 rolls for any Crap and Eleven on the Come

Out for a Progressive Bet, I list 100 plays that would be bets. Each number represents the number of intervals between winning bets:

2-3-1-1-3-12-2- (15)-7-8-8-12-2-3-6-6-24-4-6-2-6-4-11-2-12-3-4-4-1-1-7-5-1- (14)-5-1- (17)-7-7-13-6-1-1-4-9-5-12-1-9-12-3- (26)-12-10-1-5-11-2-3-5-1-4-1-5-6-7-2-5-7-1-3-1 (18)-5-1-1-3-9-12-6-3-5-3-1-5-1-1-5-1-4-1-4-3-1-2

In this list of 100 continuous bets there are only 5 intervals (nos. in parentheses) beyond the progressive limit of 12 bets which the author established. You can make your own. There were 22 winning bets after the last loss. This should satisfy anyone. To be sure 10,000 rolls of the dice requires considerable time.

This is *no play for a novice, or one with limited capital.*

Betting Seven, Eleven, Two, Three, Twelve, on the Come Out progressively is one of the surest ways of winning at Craps. In this play, as it is difficult to place your own units, it is best to stand next to the Stickman. In place of putting units on all Crap numbers, it is easier to place 2 on any Crap for 1 on Eleven. With 2 on Eleven, you have 4 on any Crap. Follow this ratio to any numbers.

In any progressive play the profits are not great, but they are very sure. To be sure, with 10 to 20 unit bets, the profit ought to satisfy anyone.

To get your play well in hand, play ten-cent chips or twenty-five-cent chips. It gives you more ease of mind.

33—Effemar's Master Combination Play on How to Beat the Game of Craps

(1) No one should attempt this Combination play until he has mastered all the important points brought out in the several preceding plays. This means a large amount of memory work, and the rolling of a pair of dice many thousands of times. Above all, a *record of the rolling dice* at the table should be kept. Unless one has a prodigious memory he cannot hope to succeed in a large way.

(2) As the game is such a rapid one, it is almost too much for one to play it alone, because too many good bets are overlooked. This can be seen by studying the examples given in the following pages. The play took most of the author's time watching Seven, Eleven, and any Crap, and making progressive bets with each one.

(3) As this Combination play embraces all the various features of the Layout excepting the Hardways, two or three persons, working in harmony, with equal interests, can do marvelously. Each should keep his own record of the rolling dice. One person should devote his entire attention to Seven, Eleven, and any Crap, with occasional bets on the Field, or Place bets on Six and Eight.

(4) A second person should devote his entire attention to the Field and Six and Eight, and at all times be on the lookout for indications of a Seven, so he can remove his money.

(5) A third person should play Pass–Come and Don't Pass–Don't Come according to the indication for each separate play. He can also make Place bets on Six and Eight. *Don't forget, Six and Eight are a gold mine if played according to indications.* These numbers come in frequency next to Seven, so why not make use of them?

(6) To make this Combination profitable, one should have plenty of capital, and not be afraid to use it, and never stop while losing. You are bound to win if you play according to the instructions.

(7) *The master Combination play* will include placing money on the following as the game progresses, according to indications:

Number Seven
Number Eleven
Any Crap
Don't Pass
Don't Come
Front Line–Pass
Come
The Field
Six and Eight

(8) In this play the player certainly needs "his wits about him." This is no time to be accepting "drinks on the House" if you expect to walk away with some "of their money."

(9) In every single feature of this play, the odds are against you—excepting Don't Pass. You are not matching wits against another of equal skill, but you are matching wits against Mr. Percentage. And you surely can beat him if you practice moderation, stop at the right time, or change tables, and keep a clear mind.

(10) Progression is not profitable except on numbers that pay 4-1, 15-1, as on Seven and any Crap, or on Two, Three, and Twelve. But it is best to take any Crap, as chance here is in your favor. But unless you have unlimited capital, a *stop loss* limit should be placed.

(11) In this play on Seven, Eleven, and any Crap, you cannot succeed unless you do make use of progression. To this end give close attention to the suggested methods on progression. You may work out a better one to suit your needs. The author seldom follows these tables literally into large numbers, because of winnings on Six, Eight, the Field, Don't-Come, Don't Pass.

(12) I checked 15,000 rolls of the dice to determine how many consecutive Come Outs occurred in which there was no Seven, or Eleven, or any Crap, Two, Three, or Twelve. This was important, for progression was employed with all these numbers. In the first 5,000 rolls (representing 20 hours) 15 consecutive Come Outs was the largest number, and the largest for the 15,000 rolls. *But most of this loss was made up with winnings on the other plays.*

As anything can happen to the LAW OF AVERAGES in the roll of the dice these 15 consecutive losses could happen "the first crack out of the box." But with sufficient capital this will not break one. *The loss from progressing on Seven, or any of the other numbers can be made up by wins on the others.*

(13) So the first and outstanding rule to follow in this Combination play is to bet Seven, Eleven, and any Crap on every Come Out, with 2 units on Seven, and 1 on each of the others. There are times when I do not follow this rule after the making of the Point. It all depends (with me) what number the Point is and what numbers preceded it, and how many rolls passed before the Point was made. But the making of the Point is a very important factor to watch, as it is followed frequently enough on the first or second roll by a Seven, Eleven, or any Crap, to make it worth while to give attention to it.

(14) In the following examples of Combination Plays, you will observe that frequently a Crap, or Eleven, or a double, or Nine and Ten are followed by units on Seven, or on all 3 numbers. When you have rolled 100,000 times you will see the reason for some of these bets. You will also note that in all 5 examples, the progression was mild. Only in 2 instances were 15 units placed on Seven. Only in 1 instance were 7 units played on Eleven.

(15) It is seldom one is out more than 100 units.

When you find yourself tired physically or mentally, STOP.

Caution—Above all, do not fail to place units on Eleven after every Come Out after a final Seven. More often than you think, the one you miss, is the one that wins. Fifteen to 1 is the big payoff that puts you far ahead. When you have 5, 10, or 20 units on Eleven, and it wins (for it surely will) prudence may suggest you take a rest.

EXAMPLES OF EFFEMAR'S MASTER COMBINATION PLAY

No. ______________________________

Bet	-7	-11	--A-Crap	--f	--6--8-	-P----	COME-	-D--P-	-Win--	-Lose
10	2	1	1							4
9								10		
2		1	1						7	1
9										2
7-	3	1	1						12	10
——										
2-	3	1	1						7	4
5	3	1	1							5
8					6---6				7	
8									7	
9									7	
8									7	
11										
10	2	1	1							4
5#	3									
9	4									3
5	5									4
4	6								28	5
7-	7									6
6	4	1	2						75	47
7-										7
8	5	1	2		6---6				7	8
10										
4										
6					8--8				8	
9									8	
8#									8	
6										
2										
7-	3	2	2						12	4
7-	4	2	2		6--6				111	66
6	2	2	2						12	4
9										6
6#										
5									7	
4										
7-										
6	2	2	2						130	76

Bet	7	-11-	-A-Crap-	-f	--6--8-	-P----	COME-	-D--P-	-Win-	-Lose	
8					6--6				7	6	
5											
9									7		
5											
4											
8											
12											
5	2	2	2							6	
9											
5											
9											
7-	3								12		
8	3	1	2							6	
7-					8--8					16	
									163	111	= +52
3-	4	1	2						14	5	
12-	4	1	2						14	5	
2-	4	2	1						30	5	
11#	4	1	1						15	5	
7#	4	1	2						16	3	57 rolls
											20 minutes
									141	23	Profit
											118 units

No.

Bet	-7	-11-	-A-Crap-	-f	--6--8-	-P---	COME-	-D--P-	-Win-	-Lose
5	2	2	2							6
8					5--5				5	
8										
3	2	2	2							6
10	2	2	2							6
5#										
6										
6										
5	3									3
9	3									3
3	5									5
7-	7	2	2						28	4
8	2	2	2							6
7-					5--5					10
7#	4	2	2						16	4
7#	4	2	2					10	16	4
5		2	3							5
11										
2	2	2	3						21	4

Bet	7	11	A-Crap	f	6--8	P	COME	D--P	Win	Lose
8	3	2	2							7
11										
7-	4	2	3						10	
									16	5
									112	78
8	4	3	3		6--6					10
8									7	
8					8--8				7	
6	4	3	2						9	9
3	5	3	2							10
10										
9										
7-	5								20	
									155	107
7#	2	2	2						8	4
6					5					
6"									6	
10	2	2	3							7
8										
5										
6										
10#	2	2	3							7
10										
11	4	2	3						30	7
7-	4	2	3						16	7
									215	139
6	3	2	3		6--6					11
12										
2	3	2	3						21	5
3										
7-	4	2	1						16	3
12-	2	2	2						14	4
7#	2	2	2						8	4
8	2	2	2							6
9										
9										
9	3	2	2							7
									274	179 = + 95 un
								forward	95	
3	4	2	2						14	4
8#	4	2	2							8
8										
8"	5	2	2							9
8										

Bet	7	11	A-Crap	f	6--8	P	COME	D--P	Win	Lose	
9	7	2	2							11	65 rolls
3	9									9	
11	11	2	2						30	13	half hour
8	8	2	3							13	
8	8	2	3							16	
4	11	2	3								Profit
8											91 units
10	13	3	3							19	
7-	15	3	3						60	6	
									199	108	

Bet	7	11	A-Crap	f	6--8	P	COME	D--P	Win	Lose	
11#	4	7	3						105	7	
8	4	2	3							9	
5					5--				[illegible]		
8#									6		37 rolls
8	2	2	3							7	
7-	3								12		20 minutes
10	2	2	3	5					5	7	
4											
9				5					5		Profit
8				5						5	
9				5					5		111 units
4											
5	2	2	3							7	
8					5--				6		
6											
9											
7-					5--5						
6									6		
11											
6#											
8	2	2	2							6	
11											
6	3									3	
5	4	2	2							8	
7-											
2-	5	2	2						14	7	
7+	5	2	2						20	4	
9	5	2	2							9	
7-											
9		2								2	
5											
4											

Bet	7	11	A-Crap	f	6--8	P	COME	D--P	Win	Lose	
2	2	2	2						14	4	
8											
5											
11											
7-									12	4	
									210	89	
7-	2	1	1						8	2	(4)
6	2	1	1		5--5					4	
7-										10	
7#								10			
4								10		10	
7-								10		10	
9										10	
5					5--5					10	
8									6		
6									6		
6									6		
4									6		
5									6		
8										10	
6											
7-											
9	4	5	2							11	
8								10			
5											
4											
10											
5											
8									10		
7-											
9	4	5	2							11	
8											
4											
10											
5											
8											
7-											
12-	5	6	3						21	11	
3-	3	6	3						21	9	
7#	5	6	2						20	8	
6	7	6	2							15	
10					10--10						
9				10					10		
9											

Bet	-7	-11-	-A-Crap-	-f	--6--8-	-P----	COME-	-D--P-	-Win--	-Lose	
4				10					10		
6#											
6#	5	3	3							11	
4	5									5	
7-											
7#	7	6	3						28	9	
9	4	6	3							13	
8											
9#				10							
9									10		
4	7									7	
5											
10	4	6								10	
6	7									7	
10	7									7	
2											
6					10-10				10		
10	7									7	
11	10	3	4						45	14	
									223	221	= -2
9	10	2	4							16	
8	13									13	
7-	15								60-		
11#	3	6	4						90	7	
11#	4	2	4						30	8	65 rolls
6	7	2	4							13	
3	7	2	4						28	9	
7-	9	2	2						36	4	Profit
									244	72	172 units

Bet	-7	-11-	-A-Crap-	-f	--6--8-	-P----	COME-	-D--P-	-Win--	-Lose	
2-	3	2	3						21	5	
3-	3	2	3						21	5	5
6	3	2	2							7	
9				5						5	
7-											
10				11					10	11	
4				3						3	
7-										10	
9	2	2							10		
4				5							
9#									5	10	
11#	3	2	2						30	4	
7#	3	2	2						12	4	

Bet	7	11	A-Crap	f	6--8	P	COME	D--P	Win	Lose	
8	4	2	2							8	
10					8--8						
7-										16	
3-	5	2	2					10	14	4	
6	2	2									
6"										10	
7-											
4	5	2	3							10	
4#											
6											
12											
8											
4											
9											
11	7	2	2						30	9	
7-	7	2	2						28	4	
7#	4	2	3						16	5	
5	2	3	4							9	
5#											
10											
11											
10#											
5	3	2	4							9	
4											
7-											
9	7	2	4							13	
6											
9#											
9	7	2	4							13	
									201	150 =	+51
7	7								28		
3		2						10	79		
3-		2						10	24		
4	2	2	2					10	10	6	
7-											97 rolls-
5	2	2								4	half hour
10				5							
9									5		Profit
5#											
6	3	2	2							7	88 units
8											
10											
9	3	1	1	10					10	5	
11	4									4	

Bet	-7	-11	--A-Crap	--f	-6--8	--P----	COME	--D--P	--Win	--Lose
5	5	1	2							8
9	5	1	2							8
7-	12	1	2						12	3
11#				10					10	
5	3	1	2							6
5										
10										
7-										
4		2						10		
4#										10
2-	4	2	2						14	6
7#	5	2	2						20	4
5	2							10		2
9										
11										
9	5	2	3	5					5	10
9										
7-	5	2	3						10	
									20	5
5	7	2	3							12
6										
5#										
9	10	3	4							17
7-										
10				10					10	
5				10						10
5				10						10
11										
7-	10	3	4						40	7
6	10	3	4							17
10					10-10					
7-										20
8		3								
6										
10										
5										
9										
5										
12										
7-										
									269	181 = +88 units

34—The Big Gamblers' Paradise

A wise man of old said, "Gold is where you find it" and also "there is a vein for silver." The silver is in Las Vegas and Reno, and the big gambler (who does not gamble) will find rich deposits there to be had within the limitations of all:

THE HARDWAYS

SEVEN—pays 4-1

ELEVEN	15-1	**THREE**
TWELVE	30-1	**TWO**
SIX	9-1	**EIGHT**
FOUR	7-1	**TEN**

ANY CRAP

7-1

This is a difficult play. To succeed in it the player must have his "wits about him," be mentally quick, and nimble of finger, and quick of movement, for he has to place chips on many numbers. In addition to all this, the *sine qua non* is plenty of capital and courage to use it properly. To use it properly the player must know thoroughly the essential points in all the previous plays, *and the indications of Seven in particular.* It is Seven alone that defeats this play. If Seven only appeared once in 50 to 100 rolls, no Club could stand this play very long.

This play, if all the numbers are entered into it, is best suited to two players. One devotes his entire attention to Seven, Eleven and any Crap; and the other to the 4 Hardways and the corresponding Place bets. The Place bets take care of the more frequent rolls of "easy" Four, Six, Eight, Ten, for money placed on Hardways is taken by the "Easy Way," if that number appears first.

Unfortunately for the player, in most casinos, the Layout places all these numbers in the middle between the two ends. Often the Stickman stands right in front of this, so the player cannot place his own chips, which he should be able to do. Harold's in Reno has the most convenient Layout for the player of all the casinos, for all the Hardways other than Seven, are also placed at each end of the table. This is most convenient if one limits his Hardway plays to Six and Eight. Then he can always place chips on Big Six and Eight to take care of the Easy Ways. *In fact this is one of the best plays on the Layout.* It is easy, and the progression is simple.

One will find it worth while to place chips on all 4 of the Hardways even at the Come Out, unless a Seven is definitely indicated. A Hardways may be the first roll of the dice. The winnings of 1 play will take care of the loss of the other 3 numbers twice. Do not progress on any 1 number until it has lost 4 times. Then place 2 units. And so with the other 3 numbers. With close attention, one can pretty well carry this in his mind.

The reader's attention is called to the Hardways as mentioned on pages 49 and 50. After a recent trip to Reno, I should also like to add the following figures on the Hardways in 11,500 rolls of the dice.

Hard Four	came 228 times
Hard Six	came 285 times
Hard Eight	came 254 times
Hard Ten	came 299 times

In 4 different sets of rolls, of over 2,000 each, Hard Ten came the most times. Six came next.

So if you wish to be very conservative, play Hard Ten, progress easily on it, and you will end with a good profit. If you will play Six and Eight, as they pay 9 to 1, you will have more profit. The reader's attention is called to the following columns of figures.

THE WAY THE ELEVEN NUMBERS ARE FORMED SHOWING THE HARDWAYS

10 4-6	11 5-6	3 1-2	10 5-5	7 6-1	7 2-5	6 3-3	7 2-5
4 3-1	8 3-5	5 4-1	8 5-3	6 2-4	6 4-2	5 3-2	5 3-2
7 2-5	11 5-6	5 2-3	10 4-6	10 6-4	4 3-1	5 4-1	4 2-2
11 5-6	5 4-1	7 4-3	3 1-2	8 5-3	6 1-5	12 6-6	2 1-1
6 4-2	6 4-2	9 6-3	2 1-1	8 2-6	6 4-2	5 1-4	3 2-1
5 4-1	9 4-5	7 5-2	10 5-2	5 2-3	4 2-2	8 5-3	12 6-6
4 3-1	6 1-5	8 3-5	9 4-5	7 3-4	11 5-6	6 1-5	10 5-5
10 5-5	9 4-5	12 6-6	8 3-5	7 1-6	6 5-1	10 6-4	8 4-4
11 6-5	9 4-5	7 5-2	8 5-3	8 4-4	5 4-1	6 5-1	9 6-4
6 4-2	11 5-6	11 6-5	6 1-5	6 3-3	5 3-2	9 3-6	8 3-5
9 6-3	7 4-3	11 5-6	11 6-5	10 6-4	7 1-6	11 5-6	5 2-3
8 2-6	8 2-6	5 1-4	8 6-2	4 4-1	9 3-6	4 3-1	6 4-2
7 1-6	12 6-6	5 2-3	7 1-6	5 2-3	3 1-2	11 6-5	6 5-1
2 1-1	5 4-1	9 3-6	8 4-4	5 1-4	7 6-1	10 6-4	6 4-2
6 4-2	9 6-3	8 4-4	7 3-4	6 3-3	12 6-6	7 3-4	6 2-4
5 4-1	5 4-1	8 5-3	6 1-5	10 6-4	7 6-1	9 6-3	4 1-3
6 4-2	10 5-5	9 5-4	5 2-3	10 6-4	6 5-1	10 5-5	6 1-5
10 5-5	10 6-4	4 1-3	10 4-6	7 2-5	9 3-6	2 1-1	10 5-5
11 6-5	4 3-1	4 2-2	11 6-5	4 1-3	6 3-3	7 2-5	5 2-3
10 6-4	8 5-3	8 6-2	8 5-3	6 4-2	9 4-5	5 1-4	7 2-5
6 5-1	10 6-4	5 2-3	5 3-2	10 6-4	4 3-1	6 2-4	7 5-2
4 3-1	7 3-4	4 1-3	10 5-5	6 3-3	8 3-5	10 4-6	10 6-4
9 3-6	6 3-3	10 6-4	7 1-6	5 3-2	6 2-4	5 1-4	6 3-3
8 4-4	7 5-2	5 4-1	4 3-1	8 5-3	8 2-6	8 6-2	8 6-2
5 2-3	6 3-3	7 4-3	11 6-5	2 1-1	9 6-3	9 5-4	2 1-1
9 4-5	3 1-2	8 3-5	6 2-4	10 5-5	11 6-5	8 6-2	7 1-6
4 2-2	9 4-5	10 4-6	7 3-4	9 6-3	9 4-5	7 6-1	9 3-6
11 6-5	6 4-2	8 4-4	9 5-4	4 3-1	3 1-2	3 2-1	8 3-5
8 6-2	3 1-2	6 5-1	4 2-2	5 1-4	6 2-4	7 4-3	6 4-2
6 5-1	7 4-3	6 1-5	6 1-5	3 1-2	6 2-4	5 2-3	4 1-3
9 3-6	10 5-5	9 6-3	7 1-6	10 6-4	6 4-2	9 5-4	8 5-3
5 4-1	3 1-2	7 1-6	7 3-4	4 1-3	10 5-5	7 5-2	6 1-5
7 6-1	8 2-6	5 3-2	3 2-1	10 5-5	7 5-2	10 4-6	6 2-4
10 6-4	7 1-6	5 2-3	8 5-3	10 6-4	3 2-1	5 2-3	4 2-2
8 5-3	10 4-6	5 2-3	3 1-2	6 4-2	8 6-2	7 4-3	6 1-5
6 2-4	6 3-3	3 2-1	9 4-5	5 2-3	3 1-2	7 6-1	7 3-4
7 6-1	8 6-2	8 5-3	10 5-5	7 3-4	8 6-2	7 5-2	2 1-1
3 1-2	5 4-1	10 4-6	9 3-6	5 4-1	3 1-2		2 1-1
6 2-4	10 6-4	5 4-1	10 6-4	4 2-2	4 2-2		
7 2-5	5 4-1		5 1-4	6 5-1			
	8 6-2			7 4-3			

7 5-2	7 5-2	5 2-3	5 2-3	12 6-6	3 2-1	8 2-6	5 3-2
7 4-3	6 3-3	7 1-6	7 1-6	8 2-6	7 6-1	7 2-5	3 2-1
9 3-6	10 5-5	9 3-6	10 4-6	4 3-1	10 5-5	2 1-1	8 3-5
8 5-3	8 3-5	7 5-2	7 1-6	11 5-6	3 1-2	8 3-5	7 4-3
9 4-5	7 5-2	7 3-4	9 5-4	9 5-4	7 4-3	9 3-6	5 2-3
6 3-3	7 4-3	10 6-4	9 5-4	6 5-1	8 6-2	9 4-5	6 3-3
3 1-2	8 3-5	5 1-4	7 1-6	5 4-1	10 5-5	7 3-4	11 5-6
8 6-2	2 1-1	9 3-6	7 3-4	4 3-1	6 4-2	7 1-6	9 3-6
7 3-4	3 2-1	10 5-5	12 6-6	8 4-4	7 6-1	7 1-6	6 4-2
7 5-2	11 6-5	7 1-6	6 2-4	5 3-2	6 3-3	7 4-3	9 5-4
7 2-5	4 3-1	2 1-1	7 2-5	8 2-6	2 1-1	7 2-5	8 5-3
8 6-2	10 4-6	7 4-3	7 4-3	9 4-5	10 5-5	5 2-4	7 5-2
10 6-4	9 3-6	4 3-1	6 1-5	4 2-2	12 6-6	8 5-3	8 5-3
10 4-6	6 4-2	7 6-1	6 1-5	7 6-1	5 1-4	7 2-5	11 6-5
7 3-4	7 6-1	12 6-6	8 4-4	9 4-5	4 2-2	4 3-1	10 5-5
2 1-1	7 3-4	3 2-1	9 3-6	9 3-6	7 2-5	8 4-4	9 3-6
9 4-5	4 3-1	6 4-2	10 5-5	4 2-2	6 4-2	7 4-3	10 5-5
10 6-4	3 2-1	6 5-1	8 6-2	4 3-1	7 3-4	4 3-1	5 2-3
10 4-6	12 6-6	5 4-1	6 4-2	2 1-1	8 2-6	7 5-2	10 6-4
3 1-2	2 1-1	2 1-1	3 1-2	7 6-1	5 3-2	10 6-4	6 3-3
8 6-2	7 5-2	5 2-3	5 2-3	12 6-6	5 4-1	6 4-2	4 1-3
6 4-2	9 6-3	2 1-1	6 5-1	10 6-4	6 2-4	4 1-3	3 1-2
5 1-4	10 6-4	9 6-3	6 1-5	9 6-3	8 5-3	7 6-1	4 2-2
11 6-5	7 4-3	6 3-3	8 3-5	8 2-6	12 6-6	5 1-4	6 2-4
12 6-6	7 3-4	7 2-5	11 5-8	7 6-1	8 4-4	6 4-2	7 4-3
4 3-1	7 2-5	7 6-1	7 1-6	11 6-5	9 5-4	3 2-1	9 5-4
7 3-4	3 2-1	6 4-2	12 6-6	11 6-5	6 3-3	4 1-3	12 6-6
7 2-5	7 1-6	3 2-1	7 2-5	8 5-3	8 6-2	5 1-4	8 2-6
5 3-2	5 1-4	8 5-3	9 3-6	6 4-2	7 1-6	10 6-4	8 5-3
3 1-2	5 4-1	6 3-3	6 1-5	7 6-1	6 1-5	11 5-6	4 3-1
7 3-4	3 2-1	6 5-1	8 5-3	7 2-5	11 6-5	7 1-6	12 6-6
7 5-2	8 4-4	7 2-5	8 6-2	8 4-4	7 3-4	8 3-5	6 5-1
2 1-1	3 2-1	3 2-1	6 5-1	9 6-3	6 3-3	8 3-5	7 1-6
6 3-3	7 4-3	6 1-5	8 2-6	5 4-1	7 4-3	7 4-3	9 3-6
6 2-4	8 4-4	10 6-4	8 5-3	6 2-4	3 2-1	6 3-3	5 3-2
4 1-3	5 4-1	8 4-4	5 2-3	7 5-2	6 5-1	9 6-3	2 1-1
4 2-2	9 5-4	10 4-6	9 4-5	8 4-4	9 6-3	4 1-3	5 2-3
5 4-1	10 6-4	4 3-1	10 5-5	5 1-4	10 5-5	7 1-6	7 4-3
5 2-3	6 3-3	9 5-4	6 1-5	9 4-5	4 3-1	7 1-6	5 2-3
5 1-4	8 2-6	10 6-4	6 1-5	8 6-2	5 4-1	7 5-2	6 3-3
8 4-4	3 2-1	6 3-3	9 6-3	10 4-6	9 3-6	5 4-1	11 5-6
8 2-6	4 3-1	8 2-6	11 5-6	7 3-4	7 2-5	8 3-5	9 3-6
12 6-6		3 2-1	6 4-2			9 4-5	
		4 3-1					6 4-2

You will note that the Hardways are underscored. Note also the number of times the same figures are made in "the Easy Way." From this you can easily work out your own method of progression. Progression is absolutely necessary to come out with a good profit. Six and Eight pay 9 to 1. Here is suggested a mild progression for each number after it loses 4 times.

1-1-1-1-2-2-2-2-3-3-3-4-4-4-5-5-5-7-7-9-9.

Practice this play on a small Layout for many hours.

To the player with "big money," it is well not to try to "break the bank" at the first try. It is well to begin with small denominations, and gradually increase. It is easy to place Six and Eight Place bets, to take care of these numbers that come "the easy way," but Four and Ten are different. However, if the player has the capital for these 4 Place bets with his money on the Hardways, and makes the proper progression, he surely is "going to town." Very often when the shooter only makes 3 rolls of the dice, one may be a Hardway.

It has been frequently mentioned in this study that "almost anything can happen in the roll of the dice, in not conforming to the LAW OF AVERAGES." In other words, a large number of rolls may intervene between any 2 repetitions of the same number. That this should happen to all 4 of the Hardways at one time for more than a few minutes, is very improbable, for next to Seven, Six and Eight appear the most frequently.

For the player who possesses the prerequisites to succeed at Craps, this particular play offers the greatest rewards. "Best of luck to you."

35—A Few Rules and Condensed Suggestions

1. Two Sevens and a Crap are frequently followed by Eleven.
2. One Eleven out of every 4 appears on an average in the Come Out.
3. A Seven after the Points Six and Eight is very common, and about as frequent on the second roll.
4. A Seven is followed by Six, Eight, Eleven and a Crap more than any other numbers.
5. A Seven is so common after Twelve, or in 1 or 2 rolls, betting it can be made profitable with some progression.

6. A Seven after two Craps (and if followed by Five) is an *outstanding bet.*
7. A Seven after 2 or 3 Tens have appeared, or Nines is worth following.
8. A Seven after Eleven, Eleven, Five (or a Crap) is an *outstanding bet.*
9. A Seven after any double and a Crap is a real bet.
10. After Four, Four, Five, Five, Four, Nine, or Nine, Ten, Twelve, Eleven is common.
11. After any triple or quadruple bet Seven and any Crap.
12. If the Point is Five, Four, or Nine, and is made, look for Eleven on the Come Out.
13. If a Seven is preceded 1 to 3 rolls by a Crap or Eleven, look for the same on the Come Out.
14. If a Six or an Eight precedes a Seven, look for the same on the Come Out.
15. Bet Six and Eight after Five, but not if it is the first point.
16. One can count on Eleven coming pretty close to 2 or more Tens, or after several Fours, or 2 or 3 Sevens.
17. The best Field numbers to bet are Nine, Four, Three, Ten, Eleven and any Crap any time.
18. If Sevens are coming pretty Fast, stay off the Pass Line and play Don't Pass–Don't Come.
19. Two Elevens appear about once in 450 to 900 rolls, so do not waste your money betting every Eleven. Eleven appears after Twelve less often than after Three. However, two Elevens can come close together.
20. It is best to protect a large bet on Pass with units on any Crap.
21. Always protect a large bet on Don't Pass with units on Eleven.
22. Remember if you are betting D-P D-C a shooter seldom makes a third Point.
23. Unless you are far ahead, do not bet the Field after Five, Six, Seven, Eight. To be sure, you will lose a bet at times, but in the long run you will be ahead.
24. When a "Hot Wind" shooter is throwing Six, Eight, Five

time after time better make Come bets. Also Place bets on Six and Eight.

25. Don't Pass—Don't Come bets are most successful after a very long play, or Two or Three 6 to 15 roll plays. One often gets 2 to 6 or 8 wins.

The author wishes to state, he did not learn these points at the public Crap tables.

36—Finis

When this manuscript was first written, after making 250,000 rolls of the dice, the following was stated: "Making a profit from Craps is no pushover. It can be achieved only by much hard hard work, careful attention, and study."

Now with 1,000,000 rolls of the dice, the above statement seems mild, for anything *can happen* in the roll of the dice, in the matter of not conforming to the LAW OF AVERAGES here and there.

However, by skillful understanding one can beat the game.

Above all things, never, never become cocky and overconfident. The changing rhythm in the roll of the dice can be very disconcerting and give you a haymaker. So don't stick your neck out.

"Let him that thinketh he standeth, take heed lest he fall" is very wholesome advice to everyone—even in a Crap game.

* * * *

A prudent man foreseeth the evil,
and hideth himself; but the
simple pass on, and are punished.

Glossary

A

Ace—a single point as one spot on the dice. Two ace is a term used by a Stickman when the Number Two turns up. Some call out 3 aces, or 4 aces, for numbers 3 and 4.

B

Back of the Front-Line means, taking the odds.

Box-Boss—a Club man who sits between two stickmen—watches the game like a hawk when "big money" is being played.

Box-Boss same as Pit-Boss.

C

Cold Dice—a term used at the table when most of the players are losing their bets. In reality, it is the frequent occurrence of a Seven, and no point being made.

Come—a space marked on the Layout for the deposit of Come bets.

Come bet—a term applied to each throw of the dice after a shooter makes his point.

Come Out—the first throw of the dice made by a new shooter. It may be a Seven, Eleven, Crap, or the Point Number.

Crap—means to lose—a losing play. A gambling game of chance played with two dice. It is also a term applied specifically to the numbers 2, 3, 12. Also it is called a misout.

Cycle—a mass movement of all the dice, changing their relative position.

D

Dealer—payoff man.

Deuce—the lowest number made by 2 dice—as Two. It also means bad luck and the devil.

Dice—means a spots-die—a spot.

Don't Come—the same as Don't Pass in all factors excepting one can put his bet down after any number rolled following the Point.

Don't Pass—the opposite of Pass in a decision. Bet must be made before the Come Out.

Doubles—a term used in this book referring to two of the same number occurring in two consecutive rolls.

F

Front Line—same as Pass. Also called the Win Line.

H

Hardways—2x2, 3x3, 4x4, 5x5, so-called because of being with their less frequent combination in contrast to the Easy Way, their most frequent combination.

Hot Wind—a slang expression to represent a shooter making rolls far beyond the average—as a shooter holding and rolling the dice for 58 minutes.

Hot Dice—when the players are winning on the Front Line, Come bets, Field and Six and Eight. Same as a "Hot Wind."

L

Layout—the smooth covering of a Crap Table, always green in color, with colored figures featuring the various spaces where bets can be made.

N

Natural—a term applied to a decision made by Seven or Eleven at the Come Out, or after making the Point.

O

Odds—the favorable chances of each combination against the unfavorable chances. It varies with the different numbers according to the ways it can be made.

P

Pass—a winning decision on the Come Out by a 7 or 11, and by making the Point. A marked space on the Layout on three sides of a Crap Table.

Pit-Boss—a floor manager and overseer of the game, watching for any defective dice—placing or removing shills as needed.

Place bets—money behind Four, Five, Six, Eight, Nine, Ten, in a space on the Layout so marked.

Play—one roll of the dice, also the number of rolls from one Seven to the next Seven.

Player—one who bets in the Crap game.

Playing the odds—bets placed back of Pass, or Don't Pass, or Come.

Point—the numbers Four, Five, Six, Eight, Nine, Ten, made at the Come Out, or by subsequent throws.

R

Rhythm—a term used by this author to indicate the roll of the dice in close conformity to the number of ways each combination is made to conform to the LAW OF AVERAGES. As for instance, when a Six or Eight, repeat over and over and no Seven, they are out of rhythm.

S

Shill—a House shooter when there are few or no customers.

Shooter—one who rolls the dice. He must make a Pass bet.

Stickman—an employee who controls the roll of the dice, at same time engaging in an interesting sing-song for entertainment and added confusion. He also may act as payoff man, or gather in the lost bets. He announces the numbers as they turn up.

His is a nerve-racking job. All appear nervous, and "smoke cigarettes like devils" as soon as they leave the table. Fortunately for them, changes are made frequently.

U

Unit—a flat bet, representing any amount one wishes to use as a standard of quantity, as ten cents, one dollar, five dollars, etc.

Index